Data Processing

Volume 2 Information System

0

The M & E Handbook Series

Data Processing

Volume 2   Information
Systems and Technology

R G Anderson FCMA, MInst, AM(Dip), FMS

Sixth edition

PITMAN PUBLISHING
128 Long Acre, London WC2E 9AN

© Longman Group UK Ltd 1987

First published in Great Britain 1974
Reprinted 1975 (twice), 1976
Second edition 1978
Third edition 1979
Reprinted 1981, 1982
Fourth edition 1983
Reprinted 1983
Fifth edition 1984
Reprinted 1986
Sixth edition (2 volumes) 1987

British Library Cataloguing in Publication Data
Anderson, R.G.
    Data processing.
    ——6th ed.——(M & E handbooks,
    ISSN 0265-8828)
    Vol. 2 : Information systems and technology
    1. Management——Data processing
    I. Title
    658′.05   HD30.2

ISBN 0 7121 0697 9

Printed and bound in Great Britain.

Contents

Part eight: Information centre and decision support systems

Preface

The speed with which information technology is changing is having a great impact on business operations and administrative activities; banking, insurance, building societies, tour operators, estate agents, manufacturing and distribution, to name but a few. The evolving technology has expanded the subject of data processing beyond all bounds and this has made it necessary to produce the new edition of this established M & E handbook in two volumes.

This volume covers management information systems and related information technology and leads on from the principles and practice of data processing covered in volume 1 into the realms of information systems and their design.

Students preparing for the new CIMA paper, Information Technology Management, will find this volume ideal for their purposes as it closely follows the requirements of the syllabus. In general, this handbook should be invaluable for students preparing for all professional examinations where a knowledge of systems concepts, systems behaviour, systems analysis and design and information technology is required.

The book begins with an introduction to the concepts of information technology and systems theory, and then goes on to discuss data, database concepts and design and on-line information systems in detail. The design of information systems is then covered and is followed by a guide to selecting and installing systems which includes a cost/benefit appraisal relating the investment to the benefits derived from its use in the control and decision-making process. The nature and use of software such as spreadsheets, word processing packages and integrated accounting packages, as well as natural language, database query systems and program generators, are discussed. Information centres, decision support systems, priority decision systems, expert systems and the expert system builder are also covered.

By concentrating on the key topics of all the main information systems and technology syllabuses and ensuring that the latest developments in this fast moving field are covered, I am confident that this new edition will continue to provide students with an invaluable aid to study.

I should like to thank the following for their help.

Apricot (UK) Ltd: Provision of photographs of the XEN computer and permission to reproduce details of SuperCalc and SuperWriter from their manuals.

British Telecom: For details relating to Prestel.

The Chartered Institute of Management Accountants: Reproduction of question from past examination paper in respect of Case study 1.

City and Guilds of London Institute: Reproduction of question from past examination paper on which Case study 2 is based.

The Institute of Chartered Accountants in England and Wales: Details relating to accounting database.

Intellect Software International Ltd: Details relating to natural language database query system.

Intelligent Environments Limited: Crystal expert system builder and Deja Vu decision support software.

Mr J. E. Downs, Senior Lecturer at Manchester Polytechnic: Use of his methodology in outlining the structured approach in Chapter 14.

System C Limited: Data relating to program generator software.

Trinity Business Systems: Data in respect of Ultraplan budgeting schedules.

Work Sciences Associates: Details relating to priority decision system.

Ron Anderson 1987

Part one
Information technology

1
Information technology (1)

Nature and purpose

1. Definition of information technology. Information technology is a term which generally covers the harnessing of electronic technology for the information needs of businesses at all levels. The term 'convergence' is often used to define the merging of various aspects of electronic technology such as the use of *microcomputers* for the processing and storage of information, the application of *electronic* spreadsheets and *business modelling programs*, *word processing* for preparing standard reports and other correspondence at high speed, and *electronic mail* for transmitting messages from one office or location to another without the use of paper (using data transmission lines which link microcomputers or devices known as office information systems (OIS)) (*see* Fig. 1.1).

Information technology also embraces the use of interactive 'viewdata' database systems such as British Telecom's Prestel or private internal viewdata systems such as ICL's Bulletin. Such systems are so termed because once information has been accessed and displayed on the screen of a television the user can, for example, book hotel accommodation or order goods at a supermarket by means of a keypad. Also included in the definition are distributed processing and information systems, often organised as local area networks (LANs), which allow the interchange of information between different parts of an organisation whilst sharing central resources, such as a database supported by a mainframe, high capacity storage and high speed printing facilities. The technology also includes the use of message switching and digital PABX, facilitating both voice and data transmission, as well as electronic printing equipment. Figure 1.2 shows the spectrum of information technology.

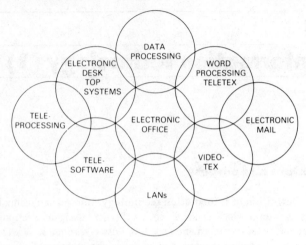

Figure 1.1 *Converging technology*

2. Information technology and modern information systems.
The viability of the electronic office was first discussed in 1947 by J. Lyons, the British catering company. As a result not only did the company apply computers to their office routines and procedures, but they actually built their own computer for the task. The computer was known as 'LEO', an acronym for Lyons Electronic Office, and became operational in 1951.

Modern information systems often incorporate mainframe computers, databases, local and wide area networks, satellite communications, electronic mail, word processing, integrated packages, spreadsheets and other decision support software. This up-to-date technology and its associated methods and techniques reduces the time information takes to flow to the various parts of an organisation, and so enables the business to conduct its activities in a more efficient manner and retain its competitiveness (*see* **3**).

Information systems in most businesses are accounting-oriented and may therefore be classed as automated accounting information systems. Other types of information systems are for controlling critical operations in real-time, i.e. whilst the operation takes place.

3. Purpose of information technology. In the context of office activities, information technology is used to improve the administra-

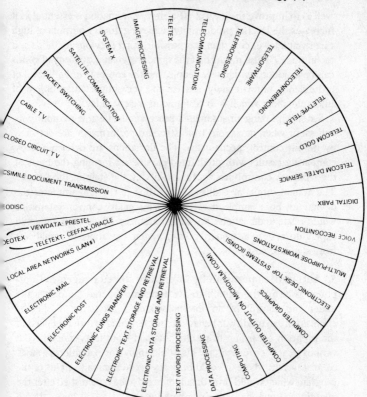

Figure 1.2 *Spectrum of information technology*

tive and managerial functions. This is largely achieved by producing information in a timely and effective manner. Information technology may therefore be considered to be the harnessing of electronic technology in its various forms to improve the operations and profitability of the business as a whole.

4. Automation in relation to information technology. The term automation is often used to describe the mechanisation of industrial operations and processes. The same principle applies to office activities as machines are being used on an ever increasing scale to reduce the ratio of administrative costs to manufacturing costs, as well as to improve the level of efficiency. Automation is essential as it increases the level of productivity, achieving greater outputs of high quality at a lower cost than was possible using previous methods and techniques. (It also means that the same or a greater quantity of goods can be produced with fewer people, and the consequent high level of redundancy unfortunately adds to the very important problem of unemployment which is to be found in society today.)

Strictly speaking an automated process must be able to modify its behaviour when deviations from standard performance are detected by inbuilt control mechanisms. The deviations are determined by comparing results with predefined parameters forming the basis of the feedback control process for modifying the state of the system. The system inputs are adjusted according to the magnitude of the deviations. For example, in respect of a budgetary control system this would relate to deviations (known as variances) of actual to budgeted expenditure, or in a standard costing system deviations of actual cost from standard cost.

5. Automatic operation by internally stored program. Computers used in the administrative functions operate automatically under the control of an internally stored program. A specific application can modify its behaviour by branching to different parts of the program according to results obtained from tests conducted at various stages of processing. This would apply, for example, in a stock control system where it would be necessary to branch to a part of the program which would print details of items to be replenished after the quantity in stock had been compared with and found lower than a predefined re-order level.

Technological life-cycle

6. Stages of the technological life-cycle. Technological changes tend to follow a predictable pattern known as the technological life-cycle. The pattern is as relevant to machines employed in the factory as it is to machines used in the office, as well as to new models of car, washing machine or television set.

The stages of the cycle are outlined below:

(*a*) introduction phase;

(b) growth phase;

(c) maturity or stability phase;

(d) decline or decay phase.

Each of these phases will now be examined in more detail.

7. Introduction phase. The introduction of new technology normally requires capital expenditure of varying magnitude depending on the nature and extent of the envisaged changes. A mainframe computer supporting local area networks can cost many thousands of pounds, and an assessment of operating and accommodation costs must be made in addition to those of a capital nature. Such costs must be related to the benefits expected to be derived from the proposed project to ensure it is a viable proposition.

The introduction phase may, for example, require the office accommodation to be restructured, or even new premises found, for a large mainframe computer installation. Internal services must then be arranged for the provision of electrical power to the various devices to be installed. This may indeed require a 'communications analysis' to be conducted to establish the optimum layout in accordance with working relationships both of personnel and equipment. (These considerations are similar to those made when installing a new automated production flow line in the factory.)

Personnel will often require retraining, especially for radical changes of equipment – 'pen pushers' are often converted to keyboard operators, particularly if concerned with multi-purpose work stations and terminals in general.

During system change-over (assuming the old system continues to function) productivity may decline because of the need for staff to be involved with both the old and new system during the implementation phase (*see* Fig. 1.3). This situation will tend to increase the operating cost per unit of output (*see* Fig. 1.4), but after the change-over it should be anticipated that unit costs will fall.

8. Growth phase. As staff become more familiar with the complexities of the new system and experience is gained, so the level of productivity should rise and the operating cost per unit fall. This will be a progressive situation until productivity stabilises at the maturity phase.

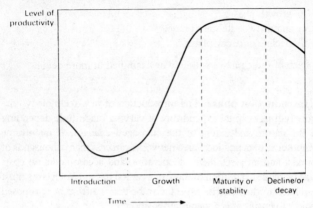

Figure 1.3   *Productivity related to stages of technological life-cycle*

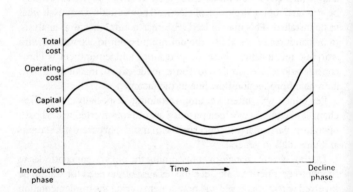

Figure 1.4   *Cost curve in relation to stages of technological life-cycle*

9.   Maturity phase. After the new system has been operational for some time it will reach its peak performance level as staff become more confident in and less apprehensive of the system. Productivity and operating costs should then stabilise at the optimum performance level.

10. Decline or decay phase. 'New' technology will eventually become outdated and machines will eventually become worn, causing system performance to decline. This is the point where the technological life-cycle returns to the introduction phase.

Machine maintenance costs, unless of a fixed nature, will become uneconomical, and the sum of the annual costs of depreciation and maintenance will increase to an unacceptable level. At this point productivity will fall as a result of machine down-time due to wear and tear and prolonged maintenance.

Part of the management of information technology is to anticipate this situation and act at the right moment to minimise system delays, increases in operating costs and low levels of performance. Management must adopt a 'forward, outward looking' stance to recognise when change is imperative to sustain or improve productivity.

Progress test 1

1. What is information technology? (**1**)

2. What are the technological characteristics of modern information systems? (**2**)

3. What is the purpose of information technology? (**3**)

4. 'The subject of information technology has a high degree of correlation with automation.' Discuss. (**4**)

5. The fundamental operation of a computer is based on an internally stored program. In what ways does this allow a computer to perform different operations at different times, i.e. modify its behaviour? (**5**)

6. State the four stages of the technological life-cycle. (**7–10**)

2
Information technology (2)

Information technology management

1. Management of innovation. Managers are agents of change, which means they must be capable of dealing with technological innovation in the quest for optimum productivity. In order to contend with this factor managers must adopt a panoramic stance, forever looking outwards as well as inwards, in order to detect both situations which warrant a change of technology and technological developments which could be harnessed to administrative activities to advantage. The management of a business must also be capable of assessing when new technology is *un*necessary since, in many instances, the use of new machines will not provide additional advantages, perhaps because existing equipment and machines serve the current needs of the business at an acceptable level of performance and cost. Attempts to implement new machines and equipment may therefore have a dysfunctional effect on the specific activities concerned incurring unnecessary costs and disruption to hitherto smooth running activities. It is also essential that departmental managers concerned with IT co-operate with systems managers responsible for managing the activities concerned with system development and implementation.

2. Elements of management. The advent of new technology does not affect the elements of management: planning, organising, controlling, staffing, directing, co-ordinating, motivating, and delegating, to which may be added problem-solving and decision-making. These apply regardless of the methodology or technology in vogue since in the final analysis it is the function of managers to manage resources, i.e. manpower, money, machines and materials of various types, used either directly or indirectly in business activities. Neither are the basic elements affected by the type of business being operated, and apply equally in a bank, insurance company, factory, warehouse, travel agency or hotel.

3. Planning. The implementation of new technology needs to be planned within the corporate framework as a whole, rather than haphazardly on the wishes of individual managers as fragmented unco-ordinated projects can have dysfunctional effects on the business. New technology should eliminate known existing organisational, systems and communication weaknesses and the problems they create as a result. These weaknesses are often due to outmoded practices and worn out machines and equipment which are not compatible with current needs. Their elimination should strengthen the business, enabling it to meet new challenges, increase productivity, reduce operating costs and streamline operations.

The inception of and change-over to a new system must be carefully planned if the system is to become operational at the target time. In order to achieve this the activities of the business must be matched with the most suitable equipment and devices, after consideration of the requirements of internal and external communications, computational and word processing needs, and the possibilities of electronic filing and electronic mail, etc.

Managers at this point need to be aware that it may be necessary to seek the advice of system specialists before drawing up more detailed plans beyond those associated with their initial ideas. The type of specialist employed depends to a great extent on whether the business already has O & M staff or systems analysts. If not, then it may be necessary to approach equipment suppliers or independent consultants, whichever seems more appropriate. Such advice should eliminate future problems and avoid a situation in which it is found that unsuitable changes have been implemented and the system has to go 'back to the drawing board'.

When a switch is made from manual or mechanically oriented systems to a sophisticated electronic system fundamental changes occur to the nature of resources used in the business: manpower tends to be replaced by machine power. The complex technological changes in an organisation may require detailed planning utilising the technique of network analysis. This requires the recording of project activities to show clearly the relationships between each event and activity. By this means the critical path can be identified, which consists of those activities which, in combination, form the longest route through the network.

Once planning has been completed and the project commences it is possible using the critical path technique to maintain effective control by identifying critical activities which, if delayed, will have an adverse effect on project completion time. On the other hand, activities with spare time available, i.e. *slack* time, allow resources to be redeployed to the critical activities thereby avoiding extending the total project time.

It may be necessary to revise original time schedules in the light of circumstances when the project is under way as it is very difficult to be precise with regard to the accuracy of the time required to perform each activity. Revisions become possible when more factual information is available during the course of the project (*see* 11:**13**).

4. Staffing. Staffing must take into account personnel policy. In the context of the management of information technology it is concerned with appointing the most suitable personnel to the new posts and retraining them when appropriate to attain the highest possible level of proficiency.

5. Organising, co-ordinating and controlling. With the implementation of new technology it may be necessary to merge what were previously separate activities or functions because of the integrative nature of some electronic devices and processes. This will necessitate the restructuring of departments, sections and tasks. This will no doubt require the span of management, i.e. the span of control, to be modified otherwise the organisation structure could be top heavy.

After changes have been implemented they must be monitored to ensure that the specified objectives are achieved, e.g. improving the speed of response to customer enquiries, or ensuring the provision of information at a specified time.

6. Motivation. The introduction of new technology may not be appreciated by all personnel. Some may be willing to accept the new ways and means of working in the hi-tech environment. Older members of staff, however, may not be very enthusiastic and are content with the present situation. They may not be very willing, or perhaps capable, of unravelling the mysteries of life in the new electronic office. Cajoling them to achieve motivation is likely to meet with little positive response.

Under all circumstances, management must be seen to be leading by example. This may require them to become keyboard conscious, and to show that they too are willing to become involved in the new way of things by direct participation.

Overcoming resistance to technological change

7. Outlook of individuals. It must be appreciated that all personnel in a business will not readily accept change for a variety of reasons, depending upon individual points of view and circumstances. Personnel, particularly those approaching retirement age, are usually content to continue with the current methods which they have become accustomed to. Consequently there is little inclination to learn new ways of doing things.

Personnel may become more enlightened and motivated if they are invited to attend informal technology meetings or participate in technology committees. In-house education and training programmes may also assist in overcoming resistance to change, particularly if personnel can see for themselves that their own area of work will benefit from the envisaged changes.

A number of situations and problems arise as a result of opposition to change including:

(a) overmanning;
(b) inefficiency;
(c) low productivity;
(d) failure to meet objectives;
(e) out-of-date methods, procedures and systems creating high processing costs;
(f) uncompetitiveness due to all of above factors.

8. Encouraging acceptance of change. There are a number of ways in which personnel may be encouraged to accept technological change. Some of these are listed below:

(a) Inform personnel affected by pending changes of the reasons for such changes.

(b) Enlist the co-operation of personnel by friendly persuasion.

(c) Allow staff to participate in the development of systems, implementing their practical ideas when appropriate.

(d) Discuss objections to change and provide genuine reasons for such change – it must not be overlooked that any changes envisaged may be to the direct benefit of personnel due to the elimination of tedious tasks.

(e) Tell the truth.

(f) Provide prestigious examples of similar changes being implemented in well-known companies.

(g) Show concern for the interests of personnel.

(h) Avoid criticising past performance.

(i) Aim at a mutually acceptable solution.

(j) Discuss, do not argue.

(k) Attempt to overcome prejudices, real or imaginary.

(l) Attempt to dispel rumours at the outset by adequate communications.

Progress test 2

1. Managers are 'agents of change'. Discuss this statement in the overall context of information technology management. (**1–6**)

2. What stance would you adopt to overcome resistance to technological change? (**7, 8**)

Part two
Systems theory

3
Outline of systems theory (1)

Spectrum of scientific principles

1. General systems theory. General systems theory (GST) provides a spectrum of scientific principles, concepts and philosophy which may be applied to the study of systems of all types. In the context of this book it embraces all types of business systems including control systems relating to quality, production, budgetary control, cost control, financial and cash control, etc. These systems provide the fabric of a management information system (MIS).

GST is based on knowledge obtained from the study of the behaviour of systems in general, including biological, mechanical, electronic and organisational systems. This encompasses the sciences of biology, physics, psychology and control engineering. Knowing the behaviour of systems under varying operating and environmental circumstances enables the behaviour of systems to be predicted to some extent. The behavioural characteristics of systems are obtained from systematic studies over a prolonged period of time, controlled experiments and by simulation. Diverse types of system often have common elements in their composition and the study of such systems generated the science of cybernetics – the science of communication and control in man and machine systems.

2. GST and long-term planning. GST implies scientific analysis of systems to obtain information of their nature, characteristics and behaviour when subjected to random influences. Long-term planning requires in-depth study (analysis) of its environment in order to detect threats and opportunities to its existence. This necessitates an analysis of the various environmental elements:

(a) economic;
(b) technological;
(c) sociological;
(d) financial;
(e) legislative.

It is then necessary to assess the extent of change in these elements in order to assess its effect on the behaviour of the business, which is essential before long-term plans can be evolved, as events in each of the various elements can create situations which prevent the achievement of objectives.

Long-term planning takes a futuristic view of the business situation, usually five to ten years ahead, for the purpose of obtaining an appreciation of all those factors which can influence the future profitability of the business. It is then possible to determine future strategy to achieve desired objectives. It is necessary to monitor (appraise) the long-term situation continuously by analysing short-term trends as the environment in which the business operates is extremely volatile and dynamic – certainly not static. Continuous appraisal also enables a business to reassess corporate strengths and weaknesses relating to capacity, finance, know-how, manpower, machines and managerial strengths, etc.

3. GST and policy-making. Policy-making is affected by GST as the relationship of external systems to the business indicates factors which must be considered when formulating the framework of company policy relating to personnel, finance, technology, marketing, production, the policy in relation to outside agencies and the public in general.

The ethical, sociological, technological and economic framework provides guidelines for establishing the internal policies of the business on the basis of which it will conduct its future operations. The corporate policies of the business mould its image as viewed by the various social groups, i.e. employees, customers, suppliers, government departments and the public generally.

The formulation of policy is the responsibility of the board of directors but it is established in consultation with managers and relevant personnel in the business. Everyone in an organisation needs to be aware of specific policies as they relate to their sphere of responsibility and authority.

4. GST and the principles of management. The principles of GST may be considered to relate to the principles of management as both are based on scientific analysis. GST is based on scientific analysis of systems to understand their nature and behaviour in varying circumstances and the effect of the environment on performance. Management principles are based on the scientific analysis of management functions and practice in various environments. It may be said, therefore, that businesses are controlled by management systems which are activated by the various control systems which themselves are based on scientific theories, i.e. GST. GST principles may conflict with the practice of management because *compromise* is often the keynote of success rather than inflexible rulings which appear relevant from previous experience. All management problems have different ingredients, which makes it impossible to pre-formulate solutions even for similar situations.

Many management problems relate to social conflict between various factions, i.e. employee–employer, customer–supplier, business–government, which do not always lend themselves to quantifiable solutions. Standard rules do not apply because they are not always acceptable by all parties to the conflict.

The nature and hierarchy of systems

5. Definition of a system. A system may be defined as a combination of interrelated elements, or sub-systems, organised in such a way as to ensure the efficient functioning of the system as a whole, necessitating a high degree of co-ordination between the sub-systems, each of which is designed to achieve a specified purpose.

If one considers the human body, it is made up of a number of related sub-systems which are interrelated and interdependent and which, as a whole, form a very powerful system which automatically adjusts its behaviour according to its environment. The human body is an adaptive system which consists of a basic framework in the form of a skeleton, a nervous system, a brain, senses relating to taste, sight, hearing and touch, as well as limbs for walking and holding objects; all co-ordinated by the central nervous system actuated by the brain.

The human body reacts to its environment in a number of ways, for instance, by shivering to keep warm when it is cold or stopping at a kerb before crossing the road.

6. Systems hierarchy. In the context of a business organisation the production function is a sub-system within the environment of a total system consisting of integrated physical and control systems. The production sub-system itself consists of smaller sub-systems in the form of machines (mechanical sub-systems) which are also interrelated with the machines' operators.

There also exist work-handling sub-systems which may be either human or automatic and the power supply sub-system, all of which interact with each other to form the hub of business operations. Physical sub-systems are governed by control or administrative sub-systems such as production control, quality control, cost control and budgetary control, etc. Information for control is generated by separately structured data processing sub-systems which are an essential element of management information sub-systems.

7. Business systems. A business system may be defined as a combination of related sub-systems consisting of a series of operations arranged in a logical sequence to achieve a particular purpose as efficiently as possible. Such systems should be standardised whenever possible and should be integrated as far as possible to achieve economy in data processing.

8. System resources. Business systems require resources to enable them to operate in the same way that a factory requires resources and, what is more, the nature of the resources required are similar for both factory and administrative systems. The difference, of course, is in the manner of their use. The major resource is finance because this is an 'enabling' resource for obtaining the other resources essential to the effective operation of systems. These resources are personnel, office space, machines and equipment and business forms and documents.

Systems relationships

9. Input/output relationships. In many cases systems have a direct relationship because, in many instances, the output from one is the input to another, even though they may be administered as separate systems. This may be due to the way in which the systems were initially developed, but in many instances input/output relationships have been the basis for integrating such systems to take advantage of administrative efficiency which larger systems often achieve.

10. Open systems. Open systems are those which interact with their environment either for the collection of information on which to base strategy, or for conducting business transactions with suppliers, customers, the general public, government departments, trade organisations, etc. Such systems adapt to changes in the environment in order to survive, which requires speedy reactions to competitive situations and other threats in the most effective way. Open systems include man, biological, organisational and business systems.

11. Closed systems. These are systems which do not interact with their environment either for the exchange of information or business transactions. Such systems are self-contained and business systems do not conform with this category as they interact with their environment to a great degree as no business exists in a vacuum.

NOTE: The reader should not confuse open and closed systems as indicated above with open-loop and closed-loop systems which are control systems.

12. Control relationships. Control systems are often separately structured from the systems which they control; for instance, the production control system controls the production quantity and the quality control system controls the production quality. In a similar manner, the cost control system controls the cost of production, and so on. These control systems are basically administrative systems for monitoring the results and modifying the state of the physical systems to which they relate.

13. Coupling and decoupling of systems (integration and disintegration). If systems are over-integrated they may become too complex to understand and operate and if one part of the system ceases to function correctly this may cause the system as a whole to deteriorate and perhaps cease to function completely. This creates unacceptable delays and disruption to those parts of the system (sub-systems) which are unable to function because of the absence of the necessary inputs from other related sub-systems.

When systems are decoupled it is easier to administer them in some cases as they become less complex and more flexible. This enables them to react to random influences as they occur without too much disruption. Decoupling may re-create the former situation whereby systems existed separately on a functional basis but were co-ordinated by the chief executive for the achievement of overall objectives. Each functional sub-system has more independence even though they are still interrelated in reality, but loosely connected for administrative convenience. Each functional executive must apply initiative to achieve functional objectives but there must also exist a high degree of co-operation between the various sub-systems to avoid sub-optimisation for the business as a whole. The efficiency with which systems are designed and integrated plays a large part in their success or failure.

Classification of systems

14. Planning systems. The purpose of some systems is to plan the operations of other systems. Planning is primarily concerned with the allocation of resources to specific tasks and the setting of performance standards. A plan establishes the guidelines for future action without which a business is likely to drift in the wrong direction. Plans set a course for the business to follow, under the guidance of the navigator, who is usually the chief executive. Plans also provide the basis for preparing budgets.

15. Mechanistic and organic systems. A mechanistic system or organisation structure is rigid in construction and is designed to operate on the basis of standardised rules and regulations which restrict its ability to react to its environment. If non-standard situations arise the system may not be able to deal with them which causes a complete breakdown of the system.

When computer systems are designed, they are usually tested by means of decision tables to ensure that all possible conditions and the relevant actions are included in the computer program. The program is then able to deal with all eventualities on the basis of defined rules. If any condition was overlooked the computer would be unable to deal with the situation until the program was modified.

It is well known that stable conditions do not exist in business for long, as the environment in which the business operates is completely fluid and interacts on the business. A mechanistic system is not sufficiently flexible to deal with such situations and is not able to adapt to the new circumstances easily. On the other hand, an organic system or organisation structure is geared to respond to environmental influences and is able to redefine its objectives according to the prevailing circumstances. It accomplishes this by an efficient re-allocation of resources and retuning of the system to the new circumstances. Mechanistic systems are also referred to as deterministic systems (*see* below).

16. Deterministic systems. Deterministic systems are mechanistic in nature and this type of system has been contrasted with an organic system to define the difference in their behaviour. It is now proposed to consider other characteristics of a deterministic system. In general, this type of system enables the output generated from specific inputs to be predicted without error. This equally applies to a computer program. Business and economic systems do not come into this category, however, as they are highly unpredictable. Mechanical systems perform in a predefined manner when subjected to specific inputs. As an example, a centre lathe behaves in a predictable manner when a specified gear is engaged (input) as it will process material at a defined speed therefore the rate of output is known. It is important to appreciate that the state of such a system can only be assessed when it is working smoothly without malfunctions and is continually under control. If wear occurs in the machine's parts then it will change its state to a probabilistic system (*see* below).

17. Probabilistic systems. Business and economic systems are of a probabilistic nature as they are subjected to random influences from the internal and external environment. It is this factor which prevents their state being predicted precisely; it is only possible to assess their probable behaviour as the effect of random variations or influences cannot be predicted with any great degree of accuracy. Indeed the occurrence of random influences themselves cannot be predicted to any great extent. The state of such systems can therefore only be defined within specified limits even when they are subject to control because stocks of raw materials, parts and finished goods, for instance, are influenced by changes in demand and variations in supply. Stock control systems are implemented to detect and control such variations on a probability basis.

Similarly, production activities are subjected to random variations in respect of manpower availability and level of productivity achieved, machine breakdowns and material supply, etc. Production planning and control systems are implemented to detect and control such variations in order to minimise their effect on the achievement of desired states.

The quality of production also varies randomly due to inconsistency in the quality of raw materials, human error and faulty machine operation. Quality control systems are designed to detect and correct such situations. At a higher level, top management cannot be sure of the outcome of any specific strategy as it is not certain what actions will be taken by competitors, suppliers, customers and the government in the future, as this depends upon the vagaries of the international economic climate at any point in time.

In general, probabilistic systems are of a stochastic nature. It is not certain what outputs will be achieved from specific inputs because it is not possible to ascertain what events will occur outside the direct control of a system which will steer it away from its desired direction or state.

18. Adaptive (self-organising) systems. This type of system is dynamic as it responds to changing circumstances by adjusting its behaviour on a self-organising basis. The system alters its inputs as a result of measuring its outputs. It attempts to optimise its performance by monitoring its own behaviour. This class of system includes animal, human and organisational systems. It is of course imperative for a business to adjust its state dynamically otherwise it would not overcome threats to its existence. This also relates to the animal world where it may be said to be the 'survival of the fittest' especially in their natural domain. Animals need to use their sensory functions to the full to detect environmental situations either to their advantage or disadvantage. It would be an appeasement of their hunger if they reacted at the right time to the availability of the right type of food in the environment. On the other hand, if the situation was reversed and they did not react to the situation where they were being hunted then the outcome could be a failure to survive.

Computerised systems such as stock control are often adaptive as changes in demand are sensed and responses are speedily implemented to change the state of the system to avoid the following.

(*a*) Overstocking and the related consequences of high average stocks, which increase the investment in stocks over the desired level, increased interest on capital, increased depreciation due to prolonged storage, increased obsolescence due to a complete fall off in demand and the increased costs of storage facilities.

(*b*) Stock shortages, which generate loss of orders or disrupt the flow of production, causing under-utilisation of resources, under-absorbed fixed overheads and loss of profits on units not produced and/or sold.

A computerised stock control system would also adjust the re-order level as a result of changes in demand to avoid re-ordering materials at a previously established re-order level. If this did not occur, then in a situation of reducing demand, a replenishment order may be placed as a result of an automatically produced re-order list which would increase the level of stock to an even higher level than required (*see* (*a*) above).

In the event of increasing demand, a failure to adjust the re-order level would mean that the program would not replenish supplies in accordance with the new circumstances and stock shortages would occur (*see* (*b*) above).

Progress test 3

1. Define general systems theory. (**1**)

2. Indicate the ways in which the process of long-term planning and policy-making could be considered to be analogous to the application of general systems theory. Your answer should include definitions of 'long-term planning and policy-making' and 'general systems theory'. (**1–3**) (*CIMA*)

3. Do you consider that the principles of general systems theory (GST) are related to the principles of management? In what way, if any, do GST principles conflict with the practice of management? (**4**) (*CIMA*)

4. Define the term 'system'. (**5–7**)

5. Specify the resources required to enable business systems to function. (**8**)

6. Indicate the nature of system input/output relationships. (**9**)

7. Indicate the nature of 'open' and 'closed' systems. (**10, 11**)

8. What are control relationships? (**12**)

9. Define the terms 'coupling' and 'decoupling' in the context of systems. (**13**)

10. One of the pitfalls a system designer must avoid is that of sub-optimality. (*a*) Define what is meant by sub-optimality and explain how it might be avoided. (*b*) Give a practical example of sub-optimality. (**13, 18**) (*CIMA*)

11. Specify the features of: (*a*) planning systems; (*b*) mechanistic and organic systems; (*c*) deterministic systems; (*d*) probabilistic systems. (**14–17**)

12. Define the nature of adaptive (self-organising) systems. (**18**)

4
Outline of systems theory (2)

The nature of organisations

1. Organisation style. Organisation style relates to the philosophy on which a business is organised and by which it arrives at decisions, and on the effectiveness of business operations. To a large extent, it is dependent upon lines of authority, delegation, working relationships and the structure of working groups.

2. Organisation theory. Organisation theory is the body of knowledge relating to the philosophical basis of the structure, functioning and performance of organisations. Such theory is derived from historical schools of thought stating the point of view of a number of early pioneers of management. Some of these are now outlined.

(a) *Scientific management.* This school of thought relates to the scientific management movement fathered by F. W. Taylor, an American engineer who sought to develop ways of increasing productivity by making work easier to perform and methods for motivating the workers to take advantage of labour-saving devices. Frank and Lillian Gilbreth made very significant contributions in the field of time and motions study and sought to improve the welfare of workers. Henry L. Gantt studied habits in industry and Harrington Emerson championed standardisation. In Germany Max Weber wrote of machinelike or bureaucratic structures where activities were formalised by rules, job descriptions and training.

(b) *Administrative management.* Paralleling the growth of scientific management was that of administrative management thought. Henri Fayol identified five universal management functions: planning, organising, commanding, co-ordinating and controlling. Fayol also developed several principles of management as guides to managerial action. Other important contributors were Mooney and Reiley who further elaborated effective organisation principles; Lyndall Urwick who helped to gather and codify early thinking on management and organisation; and Luther Gulick who contributed much in the area of public administration.

(c) *Human relations movement*. The third major school was the human relations movement. The experiments conducted by Elton Mayo at the Hawthorne plant of the Western Electricity Company in the USA revealed that an organisation was more than a formal structure or arrangement of functions. The results of his research focused attention on the behavioural approach to management and he concluded that 'an organisation is a social system, a system of cliques, grapevines, informal status systems, rituals and a mixture of logical, non logical and illogical behaviour'.

(d) *Systems approach*. The fourth school was the systems approach which sees the organisation as a total system of interconnected and interacting sub-systems, all mutually dependent. Major contributors include Trist, Bamforth, Crozier, Galbraith and Likert.

(e) *Contingency theory*. The current school is the contingency theory school which sees each organisation as a unique system resulting from an interaction of the sub-systems with the environment. The motto of contingency theory is 'It all depends'. Joan Woodware, in a study of a region's industries, found pronounced evidence that a firm's structure was closely related to its technical system of production. Other contributors to this school include Lawrence, Lorsch, Pugh, Hickson, Inkson, Child and Mintzberg.

(f) *Matrix organisation*. This is an approach to organisation design originally used by NASA and the aerospace industry which is growing in popularity. A grid or matrix of authority is established. Authority within functional departments, e.g. manufacturing, personnel and marketing, flows vertically; authority that crosses departmental lines flows horizontally. Typically the vertical flow of authority is exercised by functional managers whilst the horizontal flow is vested in project or product managers. The project or product manager is accountable for the success of a given project or product that must be processed through all or most of the functional departments. The project or product manager is thus the central co-ordinator for all activities related to a given project or product. Similar principles apply to the development of computer systems.

(g) *Mechanistic organisation.* This type of organisation is rigid in construction and is based on the hierarchical management structure. The organisation operates within the framework of procedural rules and directives designed to deal with a specified range of situations. In the real world random events occur which upset the best-laid plans. Accordingly, an organisation must be capable of dealing with them, hence the adaptive system of organisation outlined below.

(h) *Adaptive or organismic.* An adaptive system, such as a business organisation (which consists of a series of interrelated sub-systems), reacts dynamically to random influences in a self-organising manner. This is accomplished by modifying its inputs as a result of measuring its outputs and comparing them with pre-established control parameters in an attempt to optimise its performance.

Control systems

3. Definition of control system. A control system may be defined as a 'control loop' superimposed on another system having a different purpose, e.g. the production system, which is controlled by the production control system. Control is for the purpose of detecting variations in the behaviour of a system so that control signals can be communicated to the appropriate manager. He is then in a position to effect changes to the system he is managing, so that it reverts to the desired state and so achieves its objectives (*see* 9:**17**). Many administrative systems are control-oriented but they do not effect control directly – this is the prerogative of the manager concerned.

4. Basic elements of control. The basis of control in business systems consists of the following elements.

(a) *Planning.* The determination of objectives, or parameters: standard time for an operation, level of production activity required, level of sales required, expenditure allowed, performance levels required, etc.

(b) *Collecting facts.* The collection and recording of data in respect of: actual time taken, level of production achieved, level of sales achieved, expenditure incurred, actual performance level, etc.

(c) *Comparison.* The comparison of objectives with actual results for the purpose of indicating variances from planned performance in the various spheres of business operations, and informing the relevant manager of significant deviations (variances).

(*d*) *Corrective action.* Action is taken by the relevant manager (effector) to maintain a state of homeostasis (*see* 9:**17**) or to revise plans.

5. Control and the Pareto Law. An important factor for effective control is the application of the Pareto Law which, in general, states that many business situations have an 80/20 characteristic, for example, 80 per cent of the value of items in stock is represented by 20 per cent of the items. Therefore, the degree of control may be reduced by concentrating control on the 20 per cent high-value items, especially for controlling the total value of items held in stock.

Less rigid control procedures may be applied to the remaining 80 per cent of the items. Similarly, key production materials and parts may consist of 20 per cent of the total range held in stores. Therefore tight control must be applied to these items, which should reduce the number of failures to report crucial stock situations, especially if the importance of the 20 per cent is stressed sufficiently and independent checks applied to the stock records, perhaps by the stock controller or auditor.

6. Threshold of control system. The measurement of a systems output by a sensor may be defined as the keystone of control because it is the point at which control begins and is, in fact, the threshold between the physical system and the related control system. For example, the output from the factory is measured and used as a basis of control by the production control system.

7. Control interface. The communication of data from a physical system to its related control system is a means of connecting the two systems and may be defined as 'the control interface'. This may be accomplished by strategically sited data collection devices forming a factory data collection system. The data is then communicated to a computer for processing. The communication device is in fact the interface in this instance. In a more basic system the provision of source documents, such as progress tickets, to the control system serves the same purpose and may be classified as the control interface.

8. Control based on the exception principle. As can be seen above, control is often based on deviations from planned performance, which is referred to as 'management by exception'. This concept is extremely important to business control as it allows management to grasp essential facts more speedily and to correct adverse trends much sooner, owing to the fact that only significant factors are reported on. Economy is accomplished in saving on the time required to compile reports either by normal clerical methods or by computer printout. Redundancy of information is eliminated – a feature of detailed schedules in some cases, as, very often, too much information is provided for the control process. Also, detailed schedules often leave the task of filtering essential requirements to management which slows down the process of corrective action. Indeed, corrective action may not be taken at all as it is very easy for a manager to overlook essential facts in the hurly-burly of daily routine.

Examples of control techniques using the exception principle are budgetary control and standard costing. Budgetary control compares actual with budgeted results periodically for the purpose of reporting to the relevant managers significant variances for their attention. While budgetary control is used for controlling overall business results, the control of costs relating to products in respect of direct material and direct labour is achieved by standard costing.

9. Requisite variety. Business systems consist of combinations of interrelated variable elements and it is the number of such elements which creates difficulty in designing effective control systems. The number of elements is a measure of a system's inherent variety and the greater the number of elements, the greater the degree of complexity.

A control system needs to be designed with the same degree of variety as the system it is to monitor, in order to allow for all possible conditions likely to arise in the operation of the system. This is a very important feature of control systems, particularly so with regard to computer-based systems, as the range of variety must be fully catered for, so far as it is economically viable to do so, as programs must contain the necessary instructions for processing data according to its classification or significance.

Before coding a computer program for a specific application a program flowchart is normally prepared which itself may be based on a decision table. The decision table is compiled to ensure that all conditions relating to data, and all necessary actions relating to such conditions, are taken fully into account during processing. The flowchart is a means of establishing the logic of computer operations and the establishment of their completeness to achieve a desired result. A decision table is therefore an aid in the preparation of a flowchart which is, in its turn, an aid to program coding.

These factors are particularly relevant to computerised exception reporting applications such as automatic stock re-ordering and credit reporting.

The effectiveness of control is dependent upon the extent to which the variable elements in the system to be controlled have been predicted and, if not included in the computer program (when relevant), are catered for by other control procedures.

Cybernetic control

10. Definition of cybernetics. The subject of cybernetics is important for control systems of all types and the basic concepts apply equally to business control systems and to man and machine systems. Cybernetics may be defined as 'the science of communication and control in man and machine systems'. The term is derived from the Greek word *kybernētēs*, the derivative of the Latin word *gubernator*, which in English may be translated as governor or controller.

11. Cybernetic control process. The cybernetic control process is identical to the process of control based on exception reporting, i.e. management by exception. The basic elements of the cybernetic control process may be analysed as follows.

(a) *Reference input.* The use of resources is planned to achieve a defined objective(s) and appropriate control parameters are established to assist their achievement. The parameters are outlined in **4** (a) and are referred to as 'reference inputs'.

(b) *Sensor (measurement of controlled variable).* Operations are undertaken and data in respect of a system's outputs is measured by a sensor which indicates the actual state of the system, i.e. the magnitude of the output signal. The measured output is referred to as the controlled variable. A sensor may be a mechanical, electronic or manual data recorder depending upon the nature of the system being controlled.

(c) *Feedback*. The output signal is then communicated by the process of feedback to the control system.

(d) *Comparator*. The comparator compares the output signal (the actual state of the system) with the desired state (the reference input). The difference between the two states is a measure of the variance or error. A comparator may be a control clerk (stock control clerk, cost clerk, budgetary control clerk), an automatic device in a machine or a computer program.

(e) *Error signal*. The error is signalled (communicated) to the effector.

(f) *Effector*. The effector adjusts the controlled variable by modifying the input of resources perhaps to increase or decrease the level of production in accordance with status of the error signal + or –. This action is to modify the behaviour of the system to achieve the reference input and obtain a state of homeostasis (*see* 9:**17**). The effector may be a manager or supervisor in the case of business systems or an automatic device in a process control system.

(g) *Modification of reference input*. It may be found that the reference inputs of a system are inaccurately defined, invalid or out of date and require to be modified to conform to the true situation.

The subject of feedback, loops and information flows is dealt with in Chapter 9.

Progress test 4

1. What is meant by 'organisation style?' (**1**)

2. Organisation theory defines the nature of organisations according to various schools of thought. Specify several such schools of thought. (**2** (*a–f*))

3. Define the nature of mechanistic and organismic types of organisation. (**2**(*g*),(*h*))

4. Specify the nature of control systems. (**3**)

5. Briefly describe the basic elements of control systems. (**4**)

6. The Pareto Law is an important factor for effective control. What is the nature of this law? (**5**)

7. Define the following terms: (a) threshold of control system; (b) control interface; (c) exception principle; (d) requisite variety. (**6–9**)

8. Define the nature of cybernetics and the cybernetic control process. (**10, 11**)

Part three
Data

5
Data concepts

Data types

1. Data defined. In the context of data processing data may be strictly defined as unprocessed information consisting of details relating to business transactions which are collected into homogeneous groups for input to a data/information processing system to produce a specific output, i.e. information. (*See* 8:**1**.)

2. Data characteristics and types. Data is input to a data processing system so that it may be converted into information. The smallest unit of definable data is known as a 'data element', examples of which are name of customer, address of supplier, employee number, stock code and quantity in stock, etc. When data processing systems are designed data elements need to be specified precisely, including the name of the element, the number of characters it contains (size of the element), the type of character whether alphabetic or numeric, and the range of values for validation purposes to ensure that data is correct before being processed. Data elements are also referred to as 'attributes' or 'fields'.

A data element is technically the logical definition of data whereas a field refers to the physical data within the element, e.g. the data element 'quantity in stock' is the name of the element which stores the actual quantity in stock. Data elements or fields are grouped together to form a record relating to a specific entity. Other terms used to define a unit of data are 'data item' and 'variable'.

The types of data with which a business is concerned may be categorised as:

(*a*) external environment data which includes matters relating to social, political and economic factors;

(*b*) competitive data which embraces details with regard to the past performance of main competitors, their present activities and future plans;

(*c*) qualitative and quantitative data relating to quality control, levels of performance, costs, overheads, profits and losses, financial strengths and weaknesses relating to cash flows and lines of credit;

(*d*) organisational data relating to manpower levels, the structure of departments including the span of control and other similar details.

(*e*) reference data such as stock control parameters.

Certain types of data are common to most businesses, particularly those relating to payroll and purchasing, but other types of data are specific to a particular type of business. One would not expect to find the same type of data in a bank, insurance company, travel organisation or building society as would be found in a manufacturing organisation.

3. Types of data related to various types of business and business systems. Examples of data relating to specific businesses and systems include those outlined below:

(*a*) *Stock control*:
(*i*)   part number, stock number or catalogue number;
(*ii*)   quantity issued from stores to various departments;
(*iii*) quantity received into stores from suppliers;
(*iv*)   quantity returned to supplier;
(*v*)   quantity returned to stores from various departments.

(*b*) *Payroll*:
(*i*)   employee number;
(*ii*)   employee name;
(*iii*) employee department;
(*iv*)   tax code;
(*v*)   national insurance number;
(*vi*)   hours worked;
(*vii*) hourly rate of pay.

(*c*) *Car hire*:
(*i*)   type of car;
(*ii*)   size of car;
(*iii*) number of seats;
(*iv*)   engine capacity;
(*v*)   registration number;

(*d*) *Credit cards*:
  (*i*)   credit cardholder number;
  (*ii*) credit cardholder name and address;
  (*iii*) credit limit;
  (*iv*) minimum payment;
  (*v*)   details of purchases;
  (*vi*) interest;
  (*vii*) remittances.

Data flow between functions

4. Arbitrary functional boundaries. Although business activities are functionalised for administrative convenience, data does not recognise these arbitrary boundaries and flows to wherever it serves a useful purpose in the organisation. This requires a detailed analysis of system relationships when systems and procedures are being designed otherwise systems will not function smoothly – if at all. It must be appreciated that the business as a whole is a complete entity comprising a number of related functions so structured to suit the operational needs of the business in pursuit of corporate goals.

5. Interfunctional data flows. It is a well known fact that data produced by one function is often used by another as a basis for taking some specific action. A despatch note produced by the warehouse, for example, is an input to the invoicing system which produces an invoice; the invoice is then input to the sales ledger system for updating the appropriate customer's account.

As a further more detailed example, consider the following in conjunction with Fig. 5.1. Before the manufacture of standard products commences in a factory the marketing function provides sales forecasts to the production planning department which uses the information to establish the quantities of the various products to be produced in specific time periods after being adjusted by current stocks. The production plans are then drawn up which provide the means for establishing the material and parts required for the production plan prior to adjustment for current stocks by the stock control department. The purchasing function is then informed of the net requirements for which purchasing schedules are required for bought out items. The schedules are used for placing forward orders

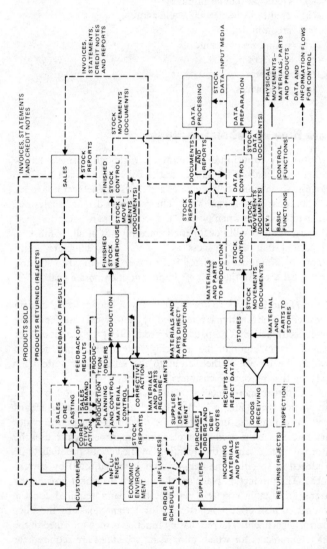

Figure 5.1 *Interfunctional data flows*

on the relevant suppliers. Sales to customers are notified to the warehouse by the sales office. The warehouse then raises despatch notes and despatches the goods to their stated destination. A copy of the despatch note (unless an integrated computerised order-entry system exists) is sent to the invoicing section of the sales office who raise a sales invoice. A copy of the invoice is sent to the customer and another to the accounts department for recording in the customer's account in the sales ledger. All such transactions are recorded in the books of account in the accounting function.

Data collection and encoding

6. Data collection and data capture. Data collection and data capture are terms concerned with the process of collecting data relating to business transactions for processing by any appropriate means but very often by computer. The primary objective is to capture data in the most economical way and to avoid having to convert it from human-sensible form to machine-sensible form if possible. This then enables the encoding stage to be eliminated.

Very often a data collection system is used for recording and transmitting data from remote locations such as branches of banks, sales offices or the offices of tour operators. This is accomplished by means of on-line terminals. In factories the modern method of capturing data employs the use of factory data recorders strategically sited throughout the factory. With this method data is captured by means of a microprocessor based terminal which allows data to be input via a keyboard, punched card or badge reader. Data is then transmitted directly to a computer.

Point-of-sale operations in supermarkets use a laser scanning technique which captures data by scanning an EAN (European Article Number) bar coded label on the goods. Data is then transmitted to an in-store computer for pricing and stock management purposes (*see* 21: **28–9** for further details of this technique).

Banks use auto-teller terminals for collecting details of cash dispensed automatically. The data collection technique adopted in this instance makes use of a keyboard to enable customers to key in their personal number and also the amount of money required. Customers are also provided with a plastic card for validating the personal number. Other methods of data capture include the use of portable computers for collecting stock control data in stores, and handprint data entry terminals which allow handprinted data to be captured and converted into ASCII code for transmission to a host computer (*see* Table 5.1).

Table 5.1. Methods of collecting and capturing data for computer input

Method/mode	Media	Data preparation/ data capture device	Input device
	Prepunched tags (Kimball tags)	Tag punch	Tag reader
Magnetic	Magnetic tape (reel)	Encoder	Tape deck
	Magnetic tape (cassette) (Key-to-cassette)	Data entry terminal/ encoder	Cassette handler
	Floppy disc (key-to-diskette)	Encoding data station	Disc unit
	Exchangeable disc pack – exchangeable disc storage (EDS) (key-to-disc)	Key stations: VDU with keyboard	Magnetic disc data transferred to magnetic tape in some systems and input to computer is via a tape deck

Table continued

Table 5.1 *continued*

Method/mode	Media	Data preparation/ data capture device	Input device
	Magnetically encoded characters: magnetic ink character recognition (MICR)	Characters printed when cheques are printed	Magnetic ink character reader/sorter
Handwritten, typed or printed optical characters	Documents prepared with optical characters: optical character recognition (OCR)	Hand, typewriter, line printer, cash register	Optical character reader
Handwritten optical marks	Documents prepared with optical marks: optical mark recognition (OMR)	Hand	Optical mark reader or Optical page reader
Handwritten normal characters	Pressure sensitive writing surface	Handprint data entry terminal	Handprint data entry terminal
Electronic sensing	Plastic card/ keyboard	Bank cashpoint terminal	Bank cashpoint terminal

Table continued

Table 5.1 *continued*

Method/mode	Media	Data preparation/ data capture device	Input device
	Plastic badge – fixed data Prepunched card – fixed data Keyboard – variable data	Factory terminal	Factory terminal
	Graphical presentation of images on video screen	Light pen	Light pen/ computer
	Graphical input of images	Graphics tablet and stylus	Stylus/computer
Electronic scanning	Bar code/ optical characters printed on label	Retail terminal equipped with low-intensity laser scanner, light pens or slot scanners	Retail terminal or cassette handler
	Bar code labels	Portable computer equipped with bar code reading wand and keyboard	Portable computer
Audio	Human voice	Audio input unit	Audio input unit
Analogue	Electronic signals	Sensor	Digitiser
Digital	Electronic signals	Terminal keyboard	Terminal

Table continued

Table 5.1 *continued*

Method/mode	Media	Data preparation/ data capture device	Input device
	Electronic signals	Terminal keyboard	Intelligent terminal
	Electronic signals	Terminal keyboard	Workstation
Electronic selection of icons	Electronic signals	Mouse	Mouse/ computer

7. Data encoding. Various data encoding methods are widely used in batch processing environments such as key-to-disc, key-to-diskette and key-to-magnetic tape. Data can then be input to a computer at a higher speed than is possible using a terminal keyboard. Direct entry of data is also widely practised in multi-user on-line processing environments which enable several personnel to process concurrently data relating to diverse applications such as payroll, invoicing, sales ledger, stock control and budgetary control, etc. (*See* Table 5.1.)

Data transmission

8. Purpose of data transmission. The primary purpose of data transmission is to transmit data from one point to another at high speed. Such facilities enable diverse operating units to communicate with each other during the course of business activities in the most efficient manner thereby eliminating unnecessary delays.

9. Modus operandi. Data transmission takes many forms, for example: remote entry of data for processing by remote job entry facilities consisting of communications oriented key-to-disc systems; on-line terminal operations; local area networks, including provision for communicating with a centralised computer supporting random enquiries by means of a corporate database. Data may be transmitted by digital signals using British Telecom's Datel, KiloStream or MegaStream services. (*See* below and Volume 1 for further details of this topic.) *KiloStream* and *MegaStream* are digital private circuit services which transmit text, data, facsimile or speech. They can also be used for slow scan visual services including closed circuit television, confravision and videostream – a video-conferencing service. KiloStream is available in various speeds including 2400, 4800 and 9600 bits per second. KiloStream Plus combines the high data rates of MegaStream with the wide availability of KiloStream. The service provides a 2 Mbits/s path providing up to 31 channels, is sited on the customer's premises and individual circuits link a number of locations. For users requiring a large number of KiloStream circuits over various routes KiloStream Plus is ideal.

MegaStream is the highest capacity digital private circuit service available from BT. It is available nationally and can be used to link high speed terminals, private branch exchanges, local and metropolitan area networks, visual services and mainframes, and voice and data can be mixed. MegaStream is ideal for corporate networks.

Data validation

10. Purpose of data validation. A computer is quite adept at processing data at an extremely high speed, and it will process erroneous data at the same speed as error-free data. It is therefore necessary to ensure data integrity by implementing routines for the detection of errors before the data is submitted for processing. It is important to appreciate that data validation is concerned with detecting recording errors on source documents, including transposed digits in reference fields, i.e. key fields. Data verification is concerned with detecting encoding errors. The initial run in a batch processing application is for the purpose of detecting and reporting on errors. This ensures that data is corrected and resubmitted before it is processed, since the processing routine contains an error control loop as shown in Figure. 5.2.

Typical data validation checks include those listed below:

(*a*)   Check to ensure that data is of the *correct type* in accordance with the program and master file.

(*b*)   Check to ensure that data is for the *correct period*.

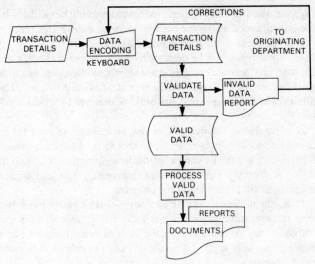

Figure 5.2 *Batch processing: data validation*

(*c*) Check to ensure that master files have the *correct generation indicator.*

(*d*) Check digit verification detects transposition errors when recording 'key' fields on source documents in respect of customer account codes, stock codes or expenditure codes, etc.

(*e*) Check to ensure that each character has the *correct number of bits* – parity check (hardware check).

(*f*) Check to ensure that records and transactions are in the *correct sequence and all are present.*

(*g*) Check to ensure that fields contain the *correct number and type of characters of the correct format* – format (or picture) check.

(*h*) Check to ensure that data *conforms to the minimum and maximum range of values,* for example, stock balances, gross wages and tax deductions, etc. As the range of specific items of data may be subject to fluctuation, the range limits may be input as parameters prior to a run instead of being incorporated in a program.

(*i*) In a nominal ledger computer application the validation of nominal ledger codes would be accomplished by reference to a nominal description file as an alternative to using check digits.

(*j*)   In an order-entry system product codes would be validated by reference to a product file and customer account codes by reference to a customer file as an alternative to using check digits.

(*k*)   Some errors may be detected by various types of check, e.g. a five-digit product code being used instead of a six-digit salesman code could be detected by a check on the type of transaction (*see* (*a*)). The difference in the number of digits could be detected by a field check (*see* (*g*)).

(*l*)   An error in the quantity of raw material being recorded in tonnes instead of kilograms could or should be detected by visual inspection rather than a computer validation program. The unit of weight is normally pre-recorded on transaction data and weight designations are predefined in the program.

(*m*)   Compatibility checks are used to ensure that two or more data items are compatible with other data items. For instance, discounts to customers may be calculated on the basis of order quantity but a discount may only apply if a customer's account balance is below a stated amount.

(*n*)   Probability checks are used to avoid unnecessary rejection of data as data can on occasions exceed normal values in a range of purely random causes. If this arises with an acceptable frequency (probability) at a defined level of confidence (normally 95 per cent), then the data need not be rejected. This would tend to reduce the level of rejections and the time expended on investigating causes of divergences.

(*o*)   Check to ensure 'hash' and other control totals agree with those generated by the computer.

Check digit verification

11. Definition. It is important to appreciate that the accuracy of output from data processing can only be as accurate as the input from which it is produced. Errors often occur in the initial recording and transcription of numerical data, such as stock numbers and account codes, frequently through transposition.

Check digit verification is a technique designed to test the accuracy (validity) of such numerical data before acceptance for processing. The data vet program performs check digit verification as part of the editing routine. Data is rejected as invalid when the check digit is any other number than the correct one. The data must then be re-encoded and re-presented for processing.

12. Check digit. A check digit is a number which is added to a series of numbers (in the form of a code number for stock or customer identification) for the purpose of producing a 'self-checking' number. Each check digit is derived arithmetically, and bears a unique mathematical relationship to the number to which it is attached. The check digit is normally added in the low-order position.

13. Modulus. Before indicating the way in which a check digit is calculated, it is necessary to understand what is meant by a 'modulus'. A modulus is the figure used to divide the number for which a check digit is required. Moduli in common use are 7, 10, 11 and 13.

14. Check digit calculation.

(a) Assume modulus 11 is selected for the purpose of calculating a check digit.

(b) Assume the number for which a check digit is required is 2323.

(c) Divide 2323 by 11 and note the remainder. Remainder is 2.

(d) Obtain the complement of the remainder and use as the check digit. 11 − 2 = 9 (complement = check digit).

(e) The number including its check digit now becomes 23239.

15. Calculation of a check digit using weights. A weight is the value allocated to each digit of a number according to a specified pattern, to prevent acceptance of interchanged digits. A more refined method of obtaining a check digit is achieved by the use of weights.

(a) Assume the same number and modulus as in the above example, i.e. 2323 and 11 respectively.

(b) The selected series of weights are 5, 4, 3, 2.

(c) Multiply each digit of the number by its corresponding weight as follows:

		Weight	*Product*
Units digit	3	2	6
Tens digit	2	3	6
Hundreds digit	3	4	12
Thousands digit	2	5	10
		Sum of products	34

(d) Divide sum of products by modulus 11 and note the remainder. Remainder is 1.

(e) Obtain the complement of the remainder and use this as the check digit: $11 - 1 = 10$ (assigned the letter **x**).

(f) The number including its check digit is 2323**x**.

A check may be applied to confirm that 10 or **x** is valid as follows:

Sum of the products	34
Add calculated check	10
	44

Divide by modulus 11 and note any remainder.

As there is no remainder, the check digit is valid.

Examples of data validation

16. Limit and range checks. For on-line processing data validation is performed interactively (*See* Fig. 5.3). This is further demonstrated by the following specimen program.

Program 1: Validation demonstrating a limit check

The example chosen here is a limit check routine on excess hours and hourly rate which could be built into a payroll system. The flowchart given in Fig. 5.4 gives rise to the program shown in Fig. 5.5 designed to trap employee hours in excess of a stated maximum and an hourly rate which does not conform to a specific value.

The interactive nature of this program is demonstrated by messages on the screen of the terminal (monitor/VDU) as follows:

Screen display	*User response*
Employee number?	Keys in employee number.
Hours worked this week?	Keys in hours worked.

If the hours worked are greater than 45 the program displays a message on the screen:

Excess hours–reinput	Keys in correct hours.

If the hours worked do not exceed 45 the program does not display this message but does display:

| Hourly rate? | Keys in hourly rate. |

If the hourly rate exceeds 2.50 the program displays a message on the screen:

| Incorrect hourly | Keys in correct rate. |
| rate–reinput | |

If the hourly rate does not exceed 2.50 then the program continues with the normal routine.

Program 2: Validation demonstrating a range check
The example chosen here is a range check to detect order quantities above or below a specified value (*see* Figs 5.6 and 5.7). Such a check could be necessary in a company in which orders less than, say, 5 need to be rejected on the grounds that the value of the order would be insufficient to cover handling costs, whereas orders over, say, 20 would be unusual and worthy of special treatment.

The interactive nature of this program is demonstrated by messages on the screen of the terminal (monitor/VDU) as follows:

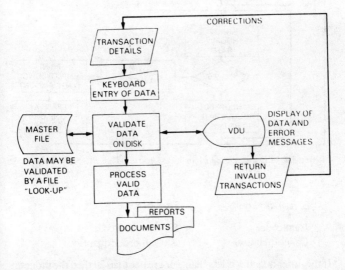

Figure 5.3 *On-line data validation*

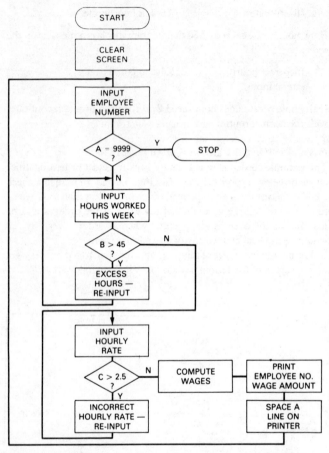

Figure 5.4 *Limit check routine on excess hours and hourly rate*

Screen display	User response
Item code?	Keys in item code.
Order quantity?	Keys in order quantity

If the order quantity is less than 5 or greater than 20 then the program displays the message:

Quantity outside range-reinput	Keys in correct quantity.

Of course quantities in excess of 20 may be correct on occasions but this is validated to ensure the integrity of the data before processing commences. The program then continues with the processing routine.

Interactive processing often incorporates 'descriptive read-back' in which a description of a part or names of customers are displayed on the screen to validate the integrity of the code numbers entered.

```
10 HOME

20 INPUT "Employee number";A

30 IF A = 9999 THEN 140

40 INPUT "Hours worked this week";B

50 IF B > 45 THEN PRINT "Excess hours-reinput"ELSE 70

60 GOTO 40

70 INPUT "Hourly rate";C

80 IF C >  2.50 THEN PRINT "Incorrect hourly

   rate-reinput"ELSE 100

90 GOTO 70

100 D = B * C

110 PRINT"Wage amount is "; D

120 PRINT

130 GOTO20

140 END
```

Figure 5.5 *Limit check program on excess hours and hourly rate*

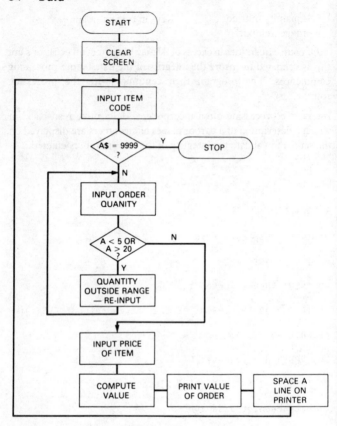

Figure 5.6 *Range check flowchart on order quantities*

Data administration

17. General considerations of batch control. It is one thing to process data, quite another to know that all the necessary data required for processing has been received, processed, errors signalled and corrections made. In order to control the flow of data in and out of the data processing system, it is normal practice to incorporate a data control section in the data processing organisation.

```
10 HOME

20 INPUT "Item code";A$

30 IF A$="9999" THEN 110

40 INPUT "Order quantity";A

50 IF A< 5 OR A > 20 THEN PRINT"Quantity outside of
   range-reinput "ELSE  70

60 GOTO 40

70 INPUT"Price of item";B

80 C=A * B

90 PRINT "Value of order for item";A$" is";C

100 GOTO 20
```

Figure 5.7 *Range check program on order quantities*

The data control section receives all incoming data for processing from internal operating departments or outlying branches. The data may already be batched when received in readiness for data preparation operations, unless the data is already in a form suitable for direct input to the computer. Each batch of data has a batch control slip attached, on which is recorded batch number, department or branch number, document count (number of documents in the batch) and other control totals if relevant such as hash or meaningful totals.

18. Recorded in register. Each batch is recorded in a register in the control section for maintaining a record of the date when the batch was received. The batches may be vetted for correctness and completeness of data in general terms and then sent to the data preparation section for encoding on magnetic tape. Data is, of course, verified to ensure the accuracy of data preparation operations before being sent for processing. After processing, the batches of documents and the printed output from the computer are sent to the data control section, where they are entered in the register as a record that all batches have been processed or otherwise. It is then necessary to check for errors discovered during processing, as outlined in **16**.

Data Protection Act 1984

19. General principles. With the wide use being made of electronic mail and databases the question of data privacy and integrity comes to the fore. This development has been recognised by the Data Protection Act 1984 which was approved by Parliament on the 12th July 1984. The Act provides that all persons in control of personal data automatically processed on computers and all providers of bureau computer services to persons in control of such data should register with the Data Protection Registrar and comply with the Data Protection Principles.

20. Principles. The Data Protection Principles apply where data users hold personal data and include the following:

(*a*) The information to be contained in personal data shall be obtained and processed fairly and lawfully.

(*b*) Personal data shall be held only for one or more specified and lawful purposes.

(*c*) Personal data held for any purpose or purposes shall not be used or disclosed in any manner incompatible with that purpose or those purposes.

(*d*) Personal data held for any purpose or purposes shall be adequate, relevant and not excessive in relation to that purpose or those purposes.

(*e*) Personal data shall be accurate and, where necessary, kept up to date.

(*f*) Personal data held for any purpose or purposes shall not be kept for longer than is necessary for that purpose or purposes.

(*g*) An individual shall be entitled at reasonable intervals and without undue delay or expense to be informed by any data user whether he holds personal data of which that individual is the subject; and to access any such data held by a data user and where appropriate, to have such data corrected or erased.

Where data users hold personal data or where relevant services are provided by persons carrying on computer bureaux, appropriate security measures shall be taken against unauthorised access to, or alteration, disclosure or destruction of, and accidental loss or destruction of personal data.

Progress test 5

1. Define the term 'data'. (**1**)

2. Specify types of data for use in various applications including stock control, payroll, car hire, credit cards. (**3**)

3. Data does not recognise functional boundaries but flows to wherever it serves a useful purpose. Discuss this statement. (**4, 5**)

4. Define the meaning of the terms 'data collection' and 'data capture'. (**6**)

5. Define the term 'data encoding' and specify two widely used encoding techniques. (**7**)

6. What is the purpose of data transmission? (**8, 9**)

7. What is the nature and purpose of data validation? How does it differ from data verification? (**10**)

8. List ten typical data validation checks that are common to most business applications. (**10**)

9. Specify the nature and purpose of check digit verification. (**11–15**)

10. Outline the interactive activities concerned with on-line validation of data relating to limit and range checks. (**16**)

11. What is the nature and purpose of data administration? (**17, 18**)

12. Define the underlying general concepts and principles of the Data Protection Act 1984. (**19, 20**)

6
Principles of database design

Database concepts

1. Definition, purpose and operating features of a database. A database may be defined as a structured collection of data supporting the whole of a business or a major business activity and consisting of a number of integrated systems. Whereas a file in a conventional functional system is a structure which links fields and records, a database is a structure which facilitates the forming of relationships between records within an application or business, removing the boundaries generally imposed by conventional files (*see* Fig. 6.1). This means that the same data may be presented in different ways to different users. (Distinction should be made between the strict definition outlined here, which is usually applicable to mainframe computers, and the way the term database is used with regard to microcomputers. In this instance there are often limitations in the degree of structure in the database and the package often provides mail-shot facilities, etc.)

The basic objective of a database is to provide up-to-date information for the effective control of business operations and for the making of decisions based on facts rather than assumptions. In addition, a database allows speedy direct access to information, and also provides efficient searching techniques which save the valuable time of executives and professional accountants, etc. When supporting software is used, such as a query language (see Natural language database query system), search techniques enable valuable information to be found which may not otherwise be possible. For example, a personnel manager may wish to be informed of personnel having specific qualifications and experience within a defined age group. This information could be extracted from the database following the

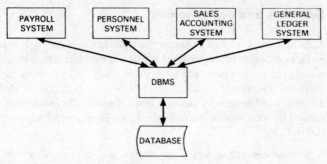

Figure 6.1 *Database file structure*

specified rules of the database software in use. The details could then be displayed or printed out as required.

Data, i.e. the content of records, must be validated by the user application programs, not by the database. System recovery should be achieved in the shortest possible time, and this is normally accomplished by dumping as frequently as possible to reduce the amount of data to be re-entered. Very often each disc is dumped as a complete unit using, for example, a VME volume copy utility for dumping disc contents to tapes. All files need to be duplexed as a fail-safe procedure against loss of data through failure of a disc or controller. Log files (or journal files in IDMS database) are frequently used in real-time/on-line update systems. All file movements, i.e. file updating transactions, are logged on a different disc to the master file or database. In the event of a system crash, the master files are recovered by recreating the master file from the last 'dump' of the file and then subsequent transactions are re-applied from the log file to bring the disc file up to date. Only fully completed transactions are recovered to avoid leaving files in an inconsistent state. Log files also provide audit trails as very often transactions have the date, time and user password/ID or terminal ID recorded against them.

2. Functional files. Files in conventional systems are designed for functional purposes. For example, a payroll system will have a payroll master file containing details of employees, i.e. employee number, name, department, tax, earnings, deductions and bank data. Some of the details may be duplicated on a personnel file with no cross reference to them. (*See* Fig. 6.2.)

Schemas and sub-schemas

3. Schemas. A schema embraces the total data in a database and includes details of how records are stored (*see* Fig. 6.3). The schema is stored in the computer and provides the basis for controlling the database. The computer needs to know how to find data in the database which is done by means of location nodes. The information derived from the schema is used by the device media control language (DMCL).

4. Sub-schemas. Sub-sets of the schema, known as sub-schemas, provide access to specific data by particular programs. For example, the stock control department will be unable to access payroll data, but the payroll department will, of course, have access to payroll data and have authority to update it. On the other hand, the personnel department will have authority to access payroll data but not to update it.

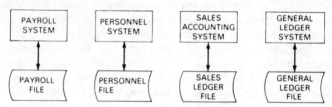

Figure 6.2 *Conventional functional files*

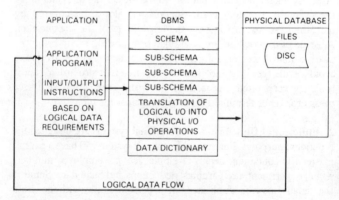

Figure 6.3 *Relationship of logical and physical data*

The sub-schema concept provides a means for the efficient control of data and facilitates data security. In addition, in some implementations, the software necessary to compile schemas is not available to application programmers. This is primarily to maintain privacy as the ability to compile schemas provides the means to bypass privacy checks.

Data and device independence

5. Data independence. Data is stored so as to achieve independence from the programs which use the data. Data structures may change without affecting programs as the structure of the data is held separately and not contained in the programs as it is for conventional processing. Because of this, programmers are not concerned with the size of data items or the way in which they are structured. It is only necessary to state the fields which are to be accessed and the DBMS presents them. If any fields are changed the only programs that will need amending are those that access them. If another field is to be added to a record, under DBMS with data independence only those programs which actually use the field will need recompiling. The operating system refers to a physical file on a specific disc but, because of the facility of data independence, this may be changed without affecting the application software using the data.

It is important to appreciate, however, that if a data structure changes this will affect the relationship between records, and the way a program navigates around the database will require modification. If, for instance, the existing 'order-item' record in the database contains the part number, then an on-line enquiry indicating a specific part number will generate a list of all current order items for that part. If the part number is removed from the order-item record and located in a part record, then the new structure will require access to the 'owner' of the part-order set, i.e. the part record, and then obtain details of order items (members) in the part-order set. All existing programs which access order items via the order-item set would have to be modified to obtain the owner of the part-order set in order to know the part being ordered. This would necessitate additional database calls (DML statements) to be inserted into the programs. This indicates the importance of effective data modelling (*see* 14:**25**), database design and normalisation to reduce structural changes after implementation.

6. Device independence. The database management system (*see* **9**) allows data to be independent of any specific file media. Individual users of specific applications still define files but the file has become a 'logical' rather than a 'physical' entity. Users cannot identify their physical functional file as being on a specific physical reel of magnetic tape or disc as was the case with separately structured files. This is because the logical data needs of every function are stored in the sub-schemas. Programs and files are not dependent upon the hardware used to hold the various files. If a file is transferred from tape to disc, or if all the files are changed from one disc type to another necessitating amendments to block length, this can be accomplished without reprogramming. Logical entities are derived from physical entities by means of database software.

Data dictionary

7. Computer-oriented catalogue. A data dictionary may be defined as a database which stores data about data in a database. It is a computer-oriented catalogue listing details and definitions of each data element, i.e. record type, file, program, system and purpose. It may also include details relating to the relationships between data elements, including functional dependencies, as well as the format and size of data elements and the minimum, average and maximum number of characters.

8. Database development. The dictionary assists in the development of a database and in reducing the level of redundancy to a necessary minimum. It also avoids duplication of data elements and facilitates easier identification of synonyms, i.e. entities having more than one name, and homonyms, i.e. one name for several entities. Details of data structures outlining the way in which data is grouped may also be incorporated in the dictionary.

Database management system (DBMS)

9. DBMS defined. A DBMS is a suite of programs which provides the database management activities. It prevents application programs from amending stored data, since updating, deletions, additions and alterations are attended to by this software by means of standard screen displays selected from options displayed in a menu. The DMBS also allows the user to validate, sort, search, update and print records from the database, and also provides facilities for performing calculations and maintaining a dictionary.

Some systems provide for the printing of standard letters and the merging of text with data such as names and addresses. Records can be displayed on the screen and browsed through, and amendments may be made as necesary. File security is achieved by making copies of disc files, and passwords may be used for data protection purposes. Files are reorganised automatically to allow for overflow conditions on disc tracks. Fields may be removed from records and files may be merged or separated according to needs.

		FIELDS		RECORDS	
TABLE	Customer No.	Name	Address	Customer	Each type of record is stored in a table, an array of rows and columns.
	565	J. B. Jones	Walsall		Rows = records.
	566	R. Smith	Bilston		Columns = fields.
					Each separate type of record has a separate table.
	Order No.	Customer No.	Date	Order	More simple to access data than a hierarchical or network structure.
TABLE	1010	565	1/1/86		Every record in the same format.
	1020	565	30/1/86		Unique key field in ascending sequence.
	1025	566	2/2/86		
	1026	566	3/2/86		
	Order No.	Product No.	Quantity	Product (order-line)	Links between the various tables are maintained by the *repeated fields*,
	1010	A	1		e.g. customer no. 565 (customer table)
	1010	B	2		appears against orders 1010 and 1020 in
	1010	C	5		order table so providing a link back to
	1020	A	2		the customer file (table).
TABLE	1020	B	3		Similarly the order no. appears in the
	1020	C	4		product table so providing a link back to
	1025	A	2		the order table.
	1025	B	1		To this extent redundancy is necessary
	1026	B	3		as the repeated fields are the only link
	1026	C	4		between tables.

Figure 6.4 *Relational database structure (sales orders)*

It is necessary to draw a distinction between DBMS used on mainframe computers such as IDMS and IMS and those relating to microcomputers which support search, update and mail shots, etc. The latter often provide only conventional file facilities and offer little in terms of 'highly structured data' (*see* **12–14** below).

Database structures

10. Integrated structure. The database approach to data storage is to consider the total data of a business as a whole and to structure that data on an integrated basis as indicated above. Specific data fields are often relevant to more than one system, but the data is entered once only to avoid the duplication which is a feature of separate functional files. This also avoids unnecessary redundancy of data thereby streamlining the database and utilising storage media effectively.

An element of redundancy in a database is unavoidable in some instances, however. For example, in a database based on a hierarchical structure (*see* **12** below) it may be necessary to refer to the same product details for different customers' orders.

11. Relational structure. This type of database structure was introduced in 1970 by Edgar Codd in order to simplify the means of gaining access to data by random requests. It is similar to the structure of a flat file (records of rigid structure) but requires specific rules for its creation.

Each type of record in the database is stored in a 'table', an array of rows and columns, the rows being the records and the columns the fields (*see* Fig. 6.4). Customer, order and product records each have a separate table. The order records may have fields relating to date, order, and customer number. By searching the orders file for those records containing specific product and customer numbers and then searching the customer file it is possible to ascertain *which* customers ordered *what* products.

The objective of a relational database structure is to make it more simple to access data than is possible using hierarchical or network database structures (*see* **12** and **13** below).

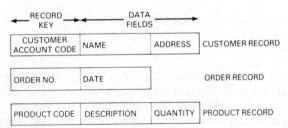

Figure 6.5 *Sales order records*

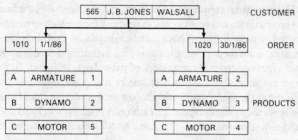

(i) The product record is repeated for each order from the same customer.

(ii) The complete structure is repeated for each order for every customer.

(iii) This structure summarises the requirements of each order.

Figure 6.6 *Sales order: hierarchical structure*

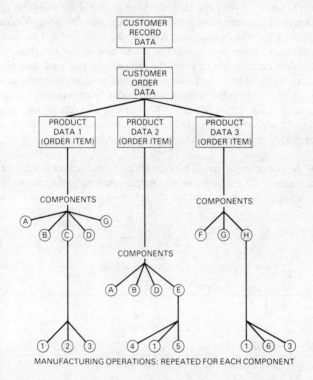

Figure 6.7 *Example of a hierarchical structure*

12. Hierarchical structure. A hierarchical structure takes the form of an inverted tree and consists of a main trunk from which stem main branches which in turn have smaller branches (sub-branches) emanating from them. The structure of the hierarchy determines the record types needed and the amount of redundancy required. In the case of customers' orders, each customer may have several orders consisting of the same product details (the product details would need to be repeated in the database for each order) (*see* Figs. 6.5 and 6.6). In addition, the structure outlined in Fig. 6.7 would be required for each customer.

The hierarchy defines the route through the database. Access starts at the top and proceeds downwards through the hierarchical structure. Each element may be related to any number of elements at any level below it but only one element above it. One of the problems of this type of structure is that cross linkages are not catered for. A sales office, for instance, would need to know the items ordered by each customer as shown in Fig. 6.5. The production control function, on the other hand, needs to know the total quantity of each product ordered from all customers because any order from any customer can consist of any one of the range of products. To obtain this information the whole database would need to be searched. The type of structure required to allow for the production of manufacturing schedules and purchasing requirements is outlined in Fig. 6.8.

13. Network structure. This type of database structure is complex and resembles the logical data relationships existing in the real world of business. It is structured around the concept of a 'set' which is a

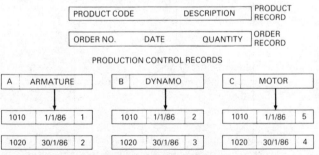

The order record is repeated for each separate order for the same product.

Figure 6.8 *Production control records: hierarchical structure*

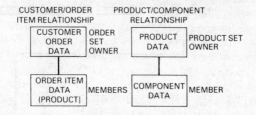

Figure 6.9 *Owner–member relationships: network structure*

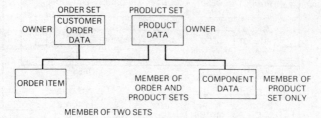

Figure 6.10 *Concept of sets: network structure*

relationship between two record types, e.g. a customer's order and an order item (*see* Fig. 6.9). An 'owner' of a set, e.g. a customer's order, can have a number of 'members', i.e. order items (*see* Fig. 6.10). A record type may be a member of several sets (*see* Fig. 6.10), an owner of several sets or a member of one set and owner of another. Sets can be incorporated without members or without owners. This can occur, for example, when new product details are introduced prior to the placing of orders or new employee details are recorded in the database prior to the first pay day. They are known as memberless sets.

The network defines the route through the database, but the user must know what linkages have been established in the database to be aware of the basis for data retrieval. Links between records are established through the use of pointers; a customer record can point to several order records which relate to it. Pointers inform the DBMS where the logical record is located. The next record is indicated by a 'next' pointer. The route through a set is first to read the 'owner' and then to access the 'members' sequentially, eventually to return to the 'owner'. It is not possible to proceed directly from the 'owner' to any specific 'member'; it is necessary to proceed via all the 'members' consecutively until the required member is reached (*see* Fig. 6.11). This is accomplished by 'next' and 'prior' pointers.

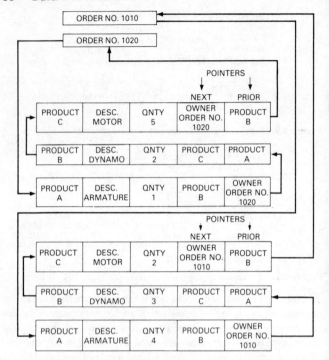

Figure 6.11 *Route through network structure illustrating next and prior pointers*

Deletions are achieved by destroying the pointers which access a record. The links between the records on either side of the one deleted are maintained by the DBMS. Insertion of records is performed by the DBMS which locates the relevant 'set' and locates the record in the most appropriate place. Data integrity is assured by an 'integrity check' utility which checks the pointers and links to ensure that sets are closed, for instance (*see* Fig. 6.12).

The database administrator

14. The database administrator as a co-ordinator. As the whole intention of a database is to rationalise business systems by the integration of such systems it follows that the data needs of an

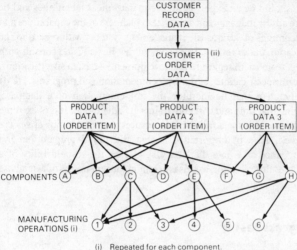

(i)   Repeated for each component.
(ii) Repeated for each customer's order.

Figure 6.12   *Network structure*

organisation must be co-ordinated at a very high level. This is basically the responsibility of a database administrator. Such a post may not yet exist in many organisations, but someone will no doubt have been vested with such responsibilities, perhaps a senior member of the systems staff.

When data is common to two or more applications then programmers are not allowed the freedom they previously enjoyed to name data elements and subject them to processing independently of other application requirements. This is where the database administrator assumes command, as it were, because he must consider the data needs of the several applications under consideration for consolidation into a database.

15. Duties of a database administrator. He must first of all be conversant with business policy and strategy, particularly for the long term, as the very fabric of a business is dependent upon an efficient and effective management information system of which a database is a fundamental part – the roots of such a system in fact. He should play an active part in the planning of information systems particularly with regard to feasibility studies.

He should be an expert in all file management techniques and be able to advise management and system planners of the capabilities and shortcomings of various file management systems with regard to the application under review. It is essential that he liaise and consult with project teams with regard to the development of design specifications, program specifications, systems documentation and programs, etc. It is imperative that he monitor the implementation of a database, ensuring that time and cost constraints are adhered to. It is of extreme importance that the administrator ensures that system objectives are achieved. Also of importance is that the initial preparation and maintenance of a data dictionary should be the responsibility of a database administrator, as this is essential for the success of a database system.

Progress test 6

1. What is a database? (**1, 2**)
2. What are schemas and sub-schemas? (**3, 4**)
3. Databases are both data and device independent. Discuss this statement. (**5, 6**)
4. Differentiate between logical and physical files in a database. (**6**)
5. Define and state the purpose of a data dictionary in the context of a database. (**7, 8**)
6. What is the nature and purpose of database software referred to as a database management system (DBMS)? (**9**)
7. Outline the features of the following database structures:

   (*a*) integrated structure,
   (*b*) relational structure,
   (*c*) hierarchical structure,
   (*d*) network structure. (**10–13**)

8. Outline the duties of a database administrator. (**14, 15**)

7
Private databases

Nature of private databases

1. Information provider and database host. Private databases are accessed via an internal network whereas public databases are nearly all accessed through the public telephone network, though most systems use the packet switch stream (PSS) network which allows users to access distant databases more economically. The data in a database is supplied by an 'information provider'. A database 'host' is the organisation which owns the computer system which supports the database supplied by the information provider for access by 'information users' who subscribe to the database.

2. Types of database. Databases may be categorised as follows:

    (*a*) private internal on-line information systems;
    (*b*) public on-line information systems provided by the host;
    (*c*) public on-line information systems provided by an information provider other than the host;
    (*d*) closed user groups;
    (*e*) home-based electronic filing systems.

Some databases may be exclusive to one host or may be available from several. Some services allow the user to take screen dumps of the information directly whereas others send copies for a stated fee. Most systems have their own specific commands but a Common Command Language is in wide use in Europe ranging over many databases.

Developments in the use of databases

3. International use. Databases are not restricted to national boundaries and there are many databases containing information of international interest in the USA and many European countries, including West Germany, Switzerland, Denmark and Luxembourg. All that is necessary for a subscriber to gain access is to dial the specific telephone number of the database.

Early databases generally only provided electronic indexing and bibliographic services, e.g. Blaise of the British Library Bibliographical Service. Other databases provided access to abstracts of papers and conference proceedings.

4. Full text services. Developments are such that full text services provide complete documents instead of abstracts. Datasolve's World Reporter provides the full text of the *Guardian, Washington Post* and *The Economist*. A full text service provided by Lexis exists for lawyers and consists of a file of legal cases relevant to the UK, US and France. The database can be searched in a variety of ways to obtain information in respect of precedents, etc.

The evolutionary development of databases provides instant information and is facilitated by on-line terminals from such sources as *The Financial Times*, the Bank of England, the IMF and the UK Treasury.

5. Searching techniques. The techniques of searching databases are continually improving, ranging from limited searches for 'key-words' acting as limited indexes to full text searching. This facility provides the means of extracting useful facts from a large volume of data which could not possibly be found by physical search methods in a short enough time, if at all. Database commands are becoming more and more powerful and the application of natural language database query systems (*see* 19: **23–29**) is increasing so that databases will be able to assist users in finding the information they are searching for.

6. Hardware and software. The hardware and software needed for accessing and retrieving information from a database include a terminal and a modem or acoustic coupler for connecting the terminal to the telephone line. When the number of the host computer is dialled the user is connected to the database. The two data transmission speeds in common use are 300 and 1200 baud. In most instances software is located at the host computer, but there are instances when the user will need to obtain software so that microcomputers may act as terminals.

7. Cost factors. Some database hosts make minimum charges. These should be considered with regard to the proposed level of use to be made of specific databases as some subscription charges are quite high. In addition, an hourly charge is made for usage which can be in the region of £30–£70 per hour. A charge is also often made for each record printed.

Telephone connect time charges or British Telecom's packet switch stream charges must also be taken into account. The PSS charges include an initial fee, a quarterly rental fee for each network user identity (NUI), i.e. a password into the system. Quarterly charges for usage appear on telephone bills and are based on usage, data volume, call duration and port holding, i.e. an hourly charge for keeping a channel connection open. In addition, costs are incurred for the purchase or rental of modems or acoustic couplers, software needs and general administration.

8. Useful addresses.

(a) *The On-line Information Centre.* This is an independent organisation providing consultancy services and publications aimed at promoting the effective use of on-line information services. The address of the Centre is: 3 Belgrave Square, London SW1X 8PL (Tel: 01-235 1732).

(b) *European Commission.* The European Commission in Luxembourg have published a useful guide entitled the *Directory of Databases and Databanks.* The address is: 177 Route d'Esch, Luxembourg.

Accounting databases

9. Accounting databases and the English ICA. Accounting databases are being developed by the English Institute of Chartered Accountants. Two working parties have been initiated, one of which covers on-line systems for taxation and the other on-line systems for other information needs. A non-tax database is available containing the following topics:

(*a*) Full numerical and textual content of the financial statements of the top 1000 public companies and building societies.

(*b*) Statements of standard accounting practice and accounting recommendations.

(*c*) Auditing standards and guidelines and other statements on auditing.

(*d*) International accounting standards, auditing guidelines and exposure drafts.

(*e*) Exposure drafts and statements of intent issued by the Accounting Standards Committee and the Auditing Practices Committee.

(*f*) Semi-authoritative material produced by the Consultative Committee of Accountancy Bodies.

(*g*) The Institute's royal charter and bylaws, guide to professional ethics and guidance for practising and non-practising members.

(*h*) Legal texts of importance to accountants such as the Companies Act.

(*i*) Authoritative texts relating to company law.

10. Further developments. The Institute is considering the following developments to the database after the initial implementation stage:

(*a*) Extension of the full text of published accounts to more companies.

(*b*) News and information releases issued by the CCAB and committees.

(*c*) Articles in magazines published by the CCAB or abstracts from them.

(*d*) Regulatory material produced by the Stock Exchange, the Bank of England, the Council of Lloyd's and other major regulating authorities in connection with accounting or reporting requirements.

(*e*) A library of qualified audit reports based on specific periodic publication of such reports.

(*f*) A software library comprising packages of particular relevance to practising accountants.

Even though the Institute's plans had not been finalised at the time of writing, the details provided above convey the probable direction of future developments. An extremely useful ICA publication is *Accountants Digest 166: On-line Information Retrieval Systems – A Guide for Accountants*.

British Standards database

11. British Standards. The British Standards Institute launched a new public database during 1986 which embraces all current British Standards. The database is stored on an external host computer to be directly accessed by means of a telephone line and a terminal. The database provides instant responses to questions and operates interactively on such aspects as newly introduced standards, amendments to standards, revisions and specifications.

The database is located at Milton Keynes and is available to members of the BSI. Members of the general public will need to contact the BSI before accessing the database. A password is provided on payment of the appropriate fee. The latest information can be obtained by ringing the following London number: 01-629 9000.

Other on-line information systems

12. Apricot UK Ltd. Apricot UK Ltd, the manufacturers of the Apricot range of computers, have a software package entitled 'Communiqué' designed to run on Apricot computers. A modem is required for connecting the computer to the telephone system and, by means of the Communiqué disc, a number of information services become available. These include:

(a) Free access to the Telecom Gold system. This electronic mail facility enables printed material to be despatched from computer to computer.

(b) Easylink provides a worldwide, low cost, telex service.

(c) Access to Prestel.

(d) Pergamon Infoline provides information on almost a million UK registered companies.

(e) Data-star or Textline provides digests of financial and business-based articles published worldwide.

(f) Extel Priceline provides the latest prices, investment ratios and share tables.

(g) Solictors and accountants are provided with a legal database, taxation details and case histories by Eurolex.

13. Official Airline Guide Electronic Edition (OAGEE). This service is available on Telecom Gold. It is a fare-based, unbiased airline flight-information system available 24 hours each day. It contains schedules relating to both direct and connecting services of over 750 airlines worldwide. The database contains details of 350,000 North American fares updated daily, 60,000 international fares updated weekly, fare price comparisons, departure and arrival times. Details are also provided in respect of airline and flight number, journey time, aircraft type, meal service and the number of stops. At the time of writing the cost of the service was 56.5 pence per minute at peak time and 38 pence per minute at off-peak time.

14. Credit control database. Dun and Bradstreet have launched a credit control database which operates on the basis of speech synthesis. (*See* Volume 1 for details of this service.)

British Telecom's Prestel

15. On-line information service. Prestel acts as host to many information providers and offers a wide range of information relating to many subjects. New databases are continuously added, details of which are published in the Prestel Directory. It is a source of on-line information but is not an information provider in its own right.

16. Viewdata and teletext. Prestel is a viewdata system operating over the telephone lines, unlike the Ceefax and Oracle teletext services of the BBC and IBA which broadcast information over the air waves in the same way as television programmes. Information is displayed on a television screen for both teletext and viewdata systems (*see* Fig. 7.1).

17. Information providers. The information on Prestel is supplied by many information providers (IPs) – in the region of 1200 in 1985. The IPs are independent organisations who rent pages from British Telecom. Some IPs, such as the Consumers' Association with its Prestel version of *Which?* magazine and Viewtel 202 with its electronic newspaper, offer information of interest to the general public. Other IPs provide services aimed at particular groups of people or organisations such as travel agencies.

Many IPs direct their information to the business world as a whole. *The Financial Times*, for example, through its subsidiary Fintel

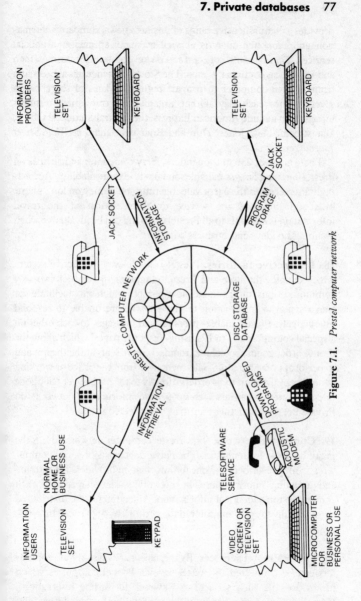

Figure 7.1. *Prestel computer network*

provides a comprehensive range of business news, company information and economic analysis as well as many specialised financial
services. *The Economist* concentrates on key statistics for businessmen
and an analysis of current events. The Stock Exchange has a direct link
from its own computer to provide regular updates of share prices
several times each day. Other organisations providing business
information include American Express, the Central Statistical Office,
Datastream, Dow Jones, Dun and Bradstreet and *The Wall Street
Journal*, etc.

There are over 250 tour operators, ferry companies and airlines on
Prestel detailing fares, timetables and up-to-date availability. Accordingly Prestel saves the agent valuable time and money on long phone
calls and improves the service to clients. Most of the travel
information is available to all Prestel users and can be invaluable when
planning holidays and business trips.

18. Interactive facilities. Prestel is a two-way interactive system
which enables the user and Prestel computer to conduct two-way
communications, unlike the teletext services which only facilitate the
transmission of information to viewers who are unable to respond
interactively. Prestel enables users to send messages to each other on
a special computer and to IPs using 'response pages' which allow the
user to order goods, book hotel rooms, reserve seats at the theatre and
to perform home banking. Salesmen away from the office or working
at home can transmit their orders directly to the office over telephone
lines. Businesses can also set up private information networks on
Private Prestel restricting their pages to selected users.

19. Computer network. The Prestel computer network covers the
major centres of population. The network consists of seven computers, six for subscribers and one for information providers for entering
and updating information. The network is star-shaped and each
computer stores identical information. Amendments are distributed
automatically to each computer in the network by high speed links (*see*
Fig. 7.1).

20. Other Prestel services. By means of gateways, private computers can be connected to Prestel sets via Prestel computers which
makes possible such services as Skytrack for airline reservations;
Homelink for home banking; Homeview for estate agents and

Viewtrade for used cars. Prestel also provides an education service for schools and Private Prestel for closed user groups.

21. CitiService. Prestel CitiService provides up-to-the-minute information from the world's financial centres for investment advisers, commodity traders and financial decision-makers. Stock market and commodity prices, foreign exchange and interest rates, unit trust prices and business and financial news and analysis are continuously updated. The service is a joint venture between Prestel and ICV Information Systems.

The latest development has been the introduction of a London Stock Exchange prices service, through a gateway, providing a continuous update facility. An interactive system known as Tax Manager enables tax computations to be performed at home on the TV screen. This service costs £2.50 for each use. Other personal financial planning services envisaged include a pensions management service and an annuities package.

Progress test 7

1. Specify the main features of private databases. (**1–14**)
2. State the primary contents of an accounting database. (**9, 10**)
3. You have been asked to prepare a report for the board of directors explaining the general features of teletext systems (e.g. Ceefax and Oracle) and viewdata systems (e.g. Prestel). Your report should also include an assessment of the likely commercial uses (if any) of these systems. (**15-21**)
4. Describe the nature of the following Prestel services:

(*a*) interactive facilities,
(*b*) gateways,
(*c*) CitiService,
(*d*) Homelink,
(*e*) Homeview,
(*f*) Viewtrade,
(*g*) Skytrack. (**18, 20, 21**)

Part four
Information

8
Information concepts

Information

1. Definition of information. Information is the output element of a data processing system. It is derived from data which has been subjected to a number of data processing operations converting related groups of related but meaningless data into a useful form for its recipients.

2. Value and nature of information. Information is the lifeblood of any business. It plays an important part in the day-to-day management of a business and the decision-making process. Information cannot be conjured out of thin air – information flows have to be designed and ingrained into the very fabric of business systems.

Information can be produced either in printed form, graphically displayed on a video screen or as graphs on a graph plotter. Printed output often takes the form of 'exception reports' or, when necessary, complete listings of the contents of a file such as the stock file, customer file, insurance file, holiday bookings file and work in process file, etc.

3. Information attributes and presentation. Managements cannot steer businesses blindly through economic and financial hazards without colliding with one obstacle or another at some stage. Information is of course needed to place them on the correct path to achieving the defined objectives of the company in the same way that the pilot of an aircraft must be guided along the correct glide path to make a safe landing, particularly in inclement weather conditions. Managers (and pilots) need information with sufficient *timeliness* to avoid any obstacles in their path as the consequences would otherwise be catastrophic, possibly leading to a crash in both instances. Desirable attributes for the effective presentation of information may be summarised as follows:

(a) It must enable management to make *effective decisions*.

(b) It must be suitable for taking *effective control action*. Or for providing valuable information relating to environmental situations.

(c) It must be compatible with the responsibilities of specific managers.

(d) It must contain an appropriate level of *detail* for the recipient.

(e) It must relate to the *current* situation.

(f) It must have an acceptable level of *integrity*.

(g) It must be compatible with *response time needs* of systems.

(h) It must be based on *exceptions* or variances to accord to the principle of management by exception when appropriate.

(i) It must be produced at an *optimum cost*.

(j) It must be easily *understandable* by the recipient.

(k) It must not contain unnecessary *redundancy*.

(l) It must be provided at a suitable *frequency*.

4. Nature of information processing. The term 'information processing' is more appropriate than the outmoded term 'data processing' as it recognises that it is 'information' which is produced as output from the processing system, not 'data'. The term 'data processing' implies that the processing of data is an end in itself rather than a means to an end.

Information processing includes all those activities which turn a set of uncorrelated facts into a meaningful correlated whole for use in the management processes of business planning, decision-making and control. The preparation of reports containing information involves subjecting the basic facts, i.e. the data, to a number of processing operations which typically include: verification (when data has been subjected to data conversion into a 'machine – sensible' form), validation, sorting, merging, computing, comparing, updating and printing. (*See* Fig. 8.1.)

5. Quantitative information. This type of information deals with the magnitude of variables, their variability and absolute value expressed in terms of the quantity of various entities. Typical examples are listed below:

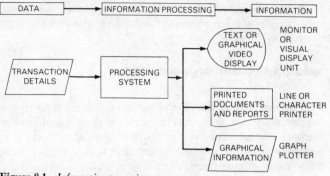

Figure 8.1 *Information processing*

(a) variations in the level of income and expenditure;

(b) variations in the level of product costs;

(c) variations from the credit limit allowed to customers;

(d) variations in the level of stocks;

(e) actual quantity produced;

(f) actual quantity sold;

(g) the level of labour turnover;

(h) average queueing time and service time in service functions;

(i) variations in the amount of capital expenditure on projects;

(j) project activity times;

(k) variations in the mix of products and the effect on profit maximisation or cost minimisation.

6. Qualitative information. This type of information relates to the attributes of an entity in respect of quality factors. Information of this nature is very useful for managerial control and often comprises comparisons with quality standards and actual achievements as a basis for 'management by exception'.

Examples of qualitative information are listed below:

(a) 'Standard of finish' of a product in respect of paintwork or electro-plating.

(b) Variations of 'tolerances' of manufactured parts, i.e. deviations from standard dimensions.

(c) Variations of 'quality' of the ingredients used in the manufacture of foodstuffs which alter taste and texture.

   (*d*) Effectiveness of 'current methods' of producing information.
   (*e*) Quality of information for effective decision-making.

Information and organisations

7. Information and the type of business. Individual businesses require information relating to the nature of their operations. For example, a car manufacturer is particularly interested in the extent of competition from overseas manufacturers and, to a lesser degree, from home based manufacturers. A tour operator is concerned about purchasing power and its effect on holiday bookings and the political situation prevailing in the various countries. The following summary will highlight the key facts required by a cross section of typical businesses to enable them to operate intelligently.

   (*a*) Car manufacturer:
      (*i*) extent of competition from overseas manufacturers;
      (*ii*) technological developments;
      (*iii*) current styling trends;
      (*iv*) success of productivity packages;
      (*v*) share of market achieved compared with that required.

   (*b*) Tour operator:
      (*i*) status of hotels in various countries and resorts;
      (*ii*) medical facilities and health hazards in various countries;
      (*iii*) political unrest in countries and its likely repercussions on holiday centres;
      (*iv*) expected level of future costs of package holidays in the light of inflationary trends and the cost of fuel for aircraft operations;
      (*v*) availability of holiday accommodation at all resorts at all times.

   (*c*) Stockbroker:
      (*i*) movement of share prices;
      (*ii*) state of money market;
      (*iii*) economic climate;
      (*iv*) climate in particular industries.

   (*d*) Building society:
      (*i*) clients overdue with mortgage repayments;

(*ii*) balances on customer investment, share and mortgage accounts;

(*iii*) likely trend in interest rates and its effect on building society funds;

(*iv*) trend in house prices;

(*v*) government policy relating to mortgage levels.

Information and the level of management

8. Top management. As a general guide, information density and volume varies according to the position of the recipient in the hierarchical management structure. For example, at the chairmanship level, information must be very broad in scope to cover the key factors which describe the economic and financial health of the business. These include profit comparisons with previous periods to obtain an appreciation of current trends so that remedial action can be taken when necessary in the most relevant way. The state of the order book is also of extreme importance as it indicates the possible level of future profits or losses which will assist in pinpointing the need for strategic decisions.

The trend of cash flows is an important key factor as it is an indicator of the financial health of the business. This will help to determine the extent to which lines of credit must be drawn upon and whether the situation indicates a need for short-term finance by way of overdraft facilities, or whether a share flotation is more appropriate for long-term growth and development.

Current share prices are also of great concern as they reflect the financial standing of the business. This has a bearing on future share flotations and the value of the business on a 'going concern' basis. Share prices also provide an indicator to possible take-over overtures.

The managing director requires similar information but also needs details of functional achievements covering the main operating areas of the business. Such information includes details of budgeted and actual income and expenditure, the latter embracing both capital and revenue, progress of contracts, jobs or projects, sales trends, level of production against targets, extent of competition measured by market share, and other information for use in corporate strategic planning and policy determination.

Much information is derived from the use of forecasting techniques and the use of spreadsheets and other modelling techniques using micros as part of decision support facilities on an end-user basis. Such techniques provide the means for assessing the viability of a number of alternative, mutually exclusive, options having inbuilt factors for assessing uncertainty and risk on a defined probability basis.

9. Functional management. This level of management requires information summaries relating to the departments for which they are responsible in sufficient detail to enable them to apply whatever measures are required to bring situations into line with requirements. For example, information will be required for the tactical planning of use of resources in order to achieve specified objectives.

Information is required which relates to current operations as they are taking place so that appropriate action can be taken to control those events while they are in progress. What has happened cannot be remedied for past periods but can, of course, be used as the basis for modifying future actions on a feedforward basis. (*See* 9: **4.**)

Depending upon the nature of the business, functional management will require details appertaining to operating expenses, manpower levels both current and projected, plant capacity, spare capacity, amount of capital expenditure incurred on various projects and the level of productivity being attained, the cost per unit of output and the incidence of scrapped production and so on. Information is often provided on an exception basis in the form of operating statements showing budgeted and actual results and variances for both the current period and for the year to date. Such statements may also include comparative figures for the same period of the previous year to indicate trends.

10. Operating or departmental management. This level of management requires information of a very detailed nature relating to specific orders, operations, personnel, materials, parts and costs, etc., because such information is essential for pinpointing areas that require some action to rectify adverse situations.

Accordingly, management needs to know about the efficiency of individuals so that direct positive action may be taken to improve it. Similarly, it is necessary to know cost variances on specific items rather than the total for all costs in order to control them. It is also necessary to know the stock position of each item in the stores to avoid unfortunate stock-out situations on the one hand and overstocking on the other. In the same context credit control can only be effective by being aware of the accounts status of individual customers.

Information for planning and control

11. Strategic planning information. Business strategy is concerned with how a company proposes to achieve its objectives. The establishment of a suitable strategy is dependent upon information relating to the company's strengths and weaknesses so that future plans can incorporate major strengths and minimise the effects of its weaknesses.

Strategy must also take into account an assessment of risk and constraints to specific courses of action. Strategic decisions often have long-range consequences, especially when concerned with the development of new products, the building of new factories and warehouses or the extending of existing premises. In these instances information is required on the available or potential market for new products, trend in building costs and development grants available for specific areas of the country and so on.

Information is also required on product life-cycles so that plans can be made to 'change-over' products at the most opportune time in order to maintain or increase profits and overall profitability. The degree of competition is always of paramount interest and information relating to market intelligence is essential. In addition, information is required in relation to developments in the economic, technological, financial, social and legal spheres so that a strategy which takes these factors into account can be formulated within the framework of company policies.

12. Tactical and operational planning information. Information for tactical planning is obtained by analysing the strategic plans into greater detail in respect of production, sales, expenditure, stocks, purchases, personnel and plant and machinery. The tactical planning activity needs to consider planning in a number of spheres, notably the planning of an effective organisation structure for achieving corporate objectives, product–market development planning, resource development planning, capital expenditure project planning and operational planning. Such plans establish the *tactics* to be employed in pursuit of strategic objectives. They are prepared by functional managers responsible for defined objectives as a means of achieving the overall objectives of the business.

13. Control information. Control information emanates from well structured, standard, routine systems including quality, budgetary, cost, credit, stock and production control systems. They all incorporate a common feature, that is 'management by exception', as they function on the basis of variances, i.e. deviations from a specified target or standard of performance. (This subject is dealt with further in 4: **8.**)

Viability of producing more information

14. Economy of producing more information. There is always a certain doubt whether the information available is sufficient for making a specific decision or whether it is economically justifiable to produce more information. It is a matter of assessing whether the quality of the decision will be increased by having more information available. It is also necessary to consider if the cost of additional information can be justified by the additional benefits derived from it.

15. Other factors to consider. It is essential for managers to be aware of the extent to which information pertaining to a specific class of decision is not available. The importance of such missing information must also be evaluated so that the manager is in a position to be conversant with the degree of risk involved and so act accordingly.

Managers should realise that it is not possible to make precise decisions on the basis of incomplete information. However, not all situations lend themselves to precise decisions because of the possibility of random influences of an unknown nature. Managers should also appreciate that they need to supplement information with experience gained in similar situations, but at the same time be aware of the different circumstances so that actions can be modified accordingly.

The nature of management information systems

16. Definitions. The Chartered Institute of Management Accountants in their booklet *Computing Terminology* define information system (or management information system) as follows:

'A computer system or related group of systems which collects and presents management information relating to a business in order to facilitate its control. The term is commonly applied to systems which make use of a database facility for the storage and retrieval of information.'

The author's definitions (contained in R. G. Anderson, *A Concise Dictionary of Data Processing and Computer Terms*, 2nd edition) are as follows:

(a) *Information system*:

'In general an information system may be defined as a data processing system which provides information to management for the purpose of controlling the business and as a basis for making decisions. Some systems incorporate a database supporting the needs of several related functions or a major operation of the business, as well as communication channels for the interchange of information between related sections of an undertaking. Some information systems are functional in nature serving the needs of specific functions. Others tend towards being a total information system, i.e. an integrated system embracing all business activities.'

(b) *Management information system*:

'Very often an MIS is based on routine data processing systems for the purpose of generating administrative documents such as payroll and payslips, invoices and statements of account, stock schedules, lists of debtors and creditors, etc. Such systems may be extended to produce various analyses for managerial control and for decision-making, particularly on the basis of reports produced on the exception principle, exception reports which notify management of essential facts. A computerised system is ideal for an MIS as it is capable of an extremely fast response-time when geared up for on-line interrogation or enquiry or even real-time control.

The objectives of MIS include the provision of information to all levels of management at the most relevant time, at an acceptable

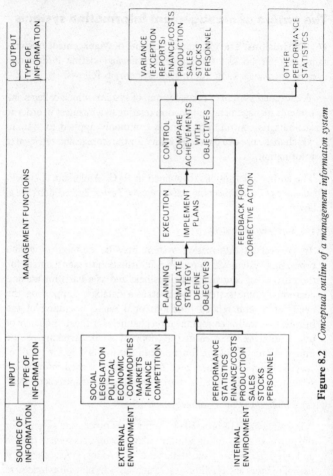

Figure 8.2 *Conceptual outline of a management information system*

level of accuracy and at an economical cost. An essential requirement of an MIS is the provision of feedback, i.e. communicating a system's measured outputs to the control system for the purpose of modifying the input to attain a state of homeostasis.' (*See* Fig. 8.2.)

17. The business operating environment. Business operations take place in a tense national and international arena, an extremely volatile environment largely consisting of random events beyond direct control in which competition is critical, profit margins are generally low and taxation is high. To overcome such formidable obstacles to the accomplishment of business objectives management are continually in need of more 'intelligence' by way of information reports so that they may run the business as effectively as possible. Information, particularly of a strategic nature, is needed to ward off threats on the one hand and to take advantage of favourable events on the other. As a consequence business management realises that to attain the utmost level of effectiveness in production, marketing and distribution, reliable information is a necessity.

In a competitive environment the business that is quick to react to changes in that environment will have a distinct advantage over its competitors. It is now appreciated that business opportunities are lost through slow communications, lost messages, lengthy searches through antiquated filing systems and other similar situations. 'Reaction time' is now tending to be reduced with the advent of modern 'information technology' which greatly improves the effectiveness of management and staff in pursuit of corporate objectives.

Corporate information adviser

18. Responsibilities of information adviser. Particularly in the larger type of organisation the post of corporate information adviser may well be considered a necessary requirement. He would be a specialist in respect of managing the information resources and requirements of the business in the same way that other managers control the use of resources connected with their activities.

The responsibilities of the post are envisaged as far-ranging, embracing all aspects of information ranging from that required for initial planning and policy formulation to the provision of information for the tactical control of operations embracing all functions: sales, production, purchasing, stock control, finance and accounting, research and development, personnel, etc. If a business is developing a database the information adviser may have the title of database administrator (*see* 6: **14–15**).

19. Co-ordinating element. An information adviser would act as a catalyst for generating all the information needs of the business and collecting information to produce cohesive reports, fully intelligible by their recipients. He should act in a consultative capacity and should conduct discussions with managers throughout the organisation for defining their specific information needs.

After the discussions have been concluded, meetings should be arranged with the data processing manager and organisation and methods manager to outline current and future information requirements. The outcome would be the establishment of priorities for the development of specific systems to produce particular information. Such systems may be computer-oriented or clerical-oriented or a combination of both depending upon volumes of data to be processed, response time needs for control and other relevant factors.

When systems are developed and ultimately implemented they should be monitored by the information adviser to ensure they are achieving their defined purpose and operating smoothly and efficiently.

Progress test 8

1.   Define and state the value of information to an organisation. (**1, 2**)

2. List twelve important attributes which information should possess for effective presentation. (**3**)

3. What is the nature of information processing? (**4**)

4. Differentiate between quantitative and qualitative information. (**5, 6**)

5. Businesses require information relating to the nature of their operations. Discuss this statement. (**7**)

6. Specify the type of information required by:

(*a*) top management,
(*b*) functional management,
(*c*) operating or departmental management. (**8–10**)

7. Specify the nature of information required for:

(*a*) strategic planning,
(*b*) tactical and operational planning,
(*c*) business control. (**11–13**)

8. State the factors to consider regarding the viability of providing more information. (**14, 15**)

9. Define the nature of management information systems. (**16**)

10. Businesses operate in a critical operating environment necessitating the need for control information to enable the business to achieve its objectives. Discuss. (**17**)

11. What are the responsibilities of a corporate information adviser? (**18, 19**)

9
Information flows, loops and feedback

Feedback concepts

1. Features of feedback. An important feature of information systems is feedback, which is the communication of a systems-measured output to a comparator for the detection of deviations (errors) (*see* Fig. 9.1).

The *Watt governor* is usually regarded as the first man-made feedback mechanism for controlling the speed of an engine.

The governor has weighted arms mounted on pivots, so that they are free to rise by centrifugal force as they revolve.

The arms turn at an increasing speed as the engine speed increases. The arms operate a valve which admits energy to the engine. The arms rise higher as the engine speed increases and the valve is closed proportionately thereby reducing the amount of energy supplied to the engine which tends to limit its speed.

If the engine fails to attain a given speed the arms are so positioned that the valve is opened more, admitting more energy until the required speed is reached. The required output (defined engine speed) is achieved by self-regulation as the input to the engine is adjusted by its own output on the feedback principle.

Self-regulation is not usually possible with business systems as the deviations from a required performance must be observed by a human being in the control system or by a computer program. Action to achieve the desired state of homeostasis (*see* **17**) must be taken by a manager after being notified of the deviations from the required state of the system. If the controller of the system fails to observe the deviations, then no effector action can take place. Even when deviations are noted and communicated to an effector he may fail to take the appropriate action.

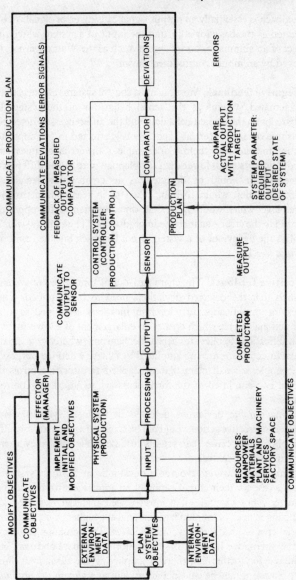

Figure 9.1 *A manual closed-loop production control system illustrating cybernetic concepts*

Feedback is essentially an output signal causing error signals to be generated as the basis for adjusting the input to a system which, in respect of an automatic control system such as the Watt governor, is achieved by an inbuilt control mechanism.

2. Negative feedback. Most business control systems are 'negative' error-actuated systems as the actual behaviour of the system is compared with the desired behaviour and the differences are detected as positive deviations (errors) and action is effected in the opposite direction to counteract them. For example, if the actual output from a production system is lower than the planned output, the difference between them would be detected as an error below standard. Corrective action would then be taken to increase output to the desired level which would necessitate an adjustment in the opposite direction to the error – an increase in production. The signal(s) which modifies the behaviour of a system is not feedback but the result of feedback (*see* **1**).

3. Positive feedback. The characteristics of some types of system are such that the detected deviations need to be amplified. The process of amplification in telecommunications is defined as a 'a unidirectional device which creates an enlargement of a wave-form'.

Amplification applies to servo-mechanisms whereby a small manual force is detected and amplified to achieve a defined purpose. For example, a small manual force applied to aircraft controls is detected and amplified to the force necessary to adjust the control surfaces.

If unfavourable deviations detected in business systems were amplified, corrective action would not be achieved as the errors would be amplified and cause the systems to deteriorate until they went completely out of control.

In situations causing favourable deviations in business systems there is a case for their amplification or an adjustment to the control parameters. For example, if a lower-priced material was used in production instead of the standard material at a higher price, then the material cost of production would be lower. This situation assumes that the alternative material is suitable for its purpose and may be considered for further use thereby amplifying the deviations. For policy reasons it may be considered prudent to maintain the original standard for a while. Alternatively, the parameter (standard) may be amended immediately, in which case the deviation will disappear completely and will not be subjected to amplification as the desired state of the system has been modified.

4. Feedforward. The error signals generated by a system are usually used to adjust the current input to a system to utilise resources more fully and to achieve system objectives. The error signals may be noted over a period of time by a monitoring process and used as a basis for planning future system resources. This approach ensures that the historical trend or inherent behaviour of a system is allowed for when establishing control parameters for future operations.

Open-loop system

5. Basic characteristics of open-loop systems. The basic characteristic of an open-loop system is that it does not contain the element of feedback. Without feedback, a system does not provide for the sensing of measured outputs for comparison with the desired outputs. Such a system does not therefore contain the element of control at all.

6. Example of open-loop system. A basic type of open-loop system could be a domestic hot-water system without a thermostat, in which case there would be no automatic regulation of the water temperature. In such a case the heater would have to be switched off manually when the desired temperature was attained.

If the heater was switched off prematurely then the desired temperature would not have been reached or, if the heater was switched off a little later, the temperature of the water would be too high. Such a system is not effective.

Within a business, control of stocks by a stock control system would not be in existence, in which case storekeepers would have to report stock shortages as they occurred which, of course, is a little late in the day to obviate the consequences of such circumstances. In addition, excessive stocks may not be noted until the year-end stocktaking by which time it is too late to take effective action to minimise losses when the excess stocks are written off or disposed of below cost.

Closed-loop system

7. Basic characteristics of closed-loop systems. An essential element of a closed-loop system is the communication of measured outputs to the control system – feedback. Such a system is defined as a closed-loop, which is a basic requirement of cybernetic systems.

Many closed-loop systems are self-regulating as they contain a built-in control mechanism, for example, the Watt governor and the thermostat in a domestic water-heating system.

Business systems containing integrated control systems performing continuous monitoring activities are also closed-loop systems as they contain the essential element of feedback (*see* Figs. 9.1 and 9.2).

8. Automatic closed-loop business systems. Computers are widely used for business data processing applications and the computer programs often contain in-built control functions. For example, a stock control application includes the processing of a transaction file and the updating of the stock master file for the purpose of calculating the new stock balance for each item in stock.

The program may also provide for the comparison of the actual quantity in stock with the maximum permissible stock and print out an 'excess stock' report for management control. The program may also incorporate automatic stock re-ordering whereby the actual quantity in stock of each item is compared with the re-order level. When the balance in stock is equal to, or less than, the re-order level a re-order list may be printed which is despatched to the purchasing department for the placing of purchase orders. Alternatively, a purchase order may be printed by the computer line printer which would reduce the lead time for the replenishment of supplies.

If, however, the balance in stock is greater than the re-order level no action is effected and the computer continues with the basic routine. The program may be defined as a built-in controller and the computer system a closed-loop system, as the actual state of the system is compared with the desired state and exception reports automatically printed (error signals).

It is essential to incorporate safeguards in this type of system which can take the form of a manual override to the action indicated by the computer program. In this way abnormal random situations not built into the computer program can be dealt with. If, for instance, there is a sudden increase or decrease in demand or supply, managerial

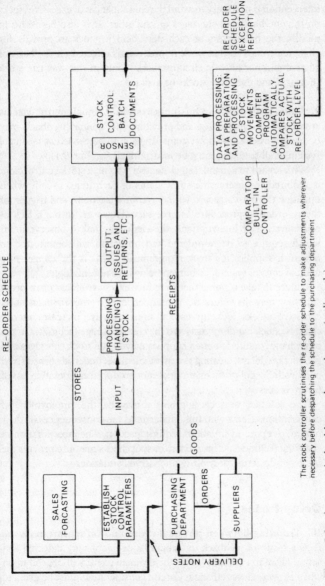

Figure 9.2 *An automatic closed-loop stock control system (outline only)*

The stock controller scrutinises the re-order schedule to make adjustments wherever necessary before despatching the schedule to the purchasing department

intervention is necessary to avoid the consequences of excessive stocks on the one hand and shortages on the other. It is also necessary to modify the parameters of each item held in stock to provide for changing trends so that stock re-ordering is effected on the basis of current and not historic circumstances – only in this way can stock shortages and excessive stocks be avoided.

9. Manual closed-loop business system. Manual control systems are widely used in business and providing they contain feedback, may be classed as closed-loop systems. Indeed, to be classed as a control system at all feedback must be incorporated (*see* Fig. 9.1).

With regard to a manual stock control system, a stock control clerk is required to observe the stock status of each item, usually when updating the master record with current transactions, and trigger off the re-ordering procedure as necessary. However, through lack of concentration or interruptions, the clerk may fail to observe items which require to be re-ordered and no action will be effected to replenish supplies for stock requirements. This is the danger of a manual control system, as human beings are not infallible.

Failure to take action either to reduce excessive stocks or re-order supplies may have drastic consequences. In the first instance, excessive stocks lock up capital unnecessarily, increase interest charges, stock handling costs and the cost of storage facilities. On the other hand, failure to obtain supplies may create stock shortages and production delays, creating excessive idle time, under-absorbed fixed overheads, loss of profit on products not produced and possible loss of future orders.

The solution to such a problem may be the employment of conscientious clerks who fully understand the consequences of their failure to report on situations requiring action. The incorporation of checking facilities such as random or spot checks may also provide the means of detecting previously unobserved situations.

Delay factor

10. Time-lag between physical event and information flows. If as a result of feedback unfavourable deviations are detected and action taken to eliminate them, the ultimate result will depend upon when the action was effected. Careful consideration must be given to the time-lag between a physical event and the information flows informing the effector of the event. For instance, if an unfavourable production output is detected and action is taken too late to alter the situation, then it is out of phase because the state of the system has probably changed in the meantime and action is taken to remedy a situation which no longer exists. This is referred to as the 'delay factor' and such circumstances cause systems to hunt or oscillate around the desired state (*see* **14**).

In the circumstances outlined, if production failed to meet the desired target, action would be taken to increase production but if the necessary adjustment was delayed it is possible that, in the meantime, production has taken an upward swing. The result of the delayed action to increase production would tend to increase production even more, perhaps to a greater level than is warranted by the previous shortfall.

An adjustment may then be effected to reduce production but by this time production may have taken a downward swing and the delayed action would decrease production below the desired level thereby amplifying the situation.

11. Amplification and damping. The principles outlined show that if action to remedy a situation is delayed then the result achieved is of a positive feedback nature, whereby deviations are amplified instead of being damped down. What was meant to be negative feedback becomes positive feedback.

12. Practical example. In order to demonstrate the above principles and concepts Table 9.1 outlines the actual production output in five different weeks, the delayed information flow in respect of each week's output, the 'corrective' action taken, and the resulting output. The table should be studied in conjunction with Fig. 9.3.

13. Timeliness of information. Other aspects of the timing of information flows and the resulting action may be related to the preparation of annual accounts and the balance sheet of a company at the end of the financial year. These are, of course, historical and, although delay in their preparation should be minimised, no action can be taken to remedy the situation disclosed even if the facts are available within one day of the year-end. The operations for the year are complete. Recognition of this situation has led to the development

Table 9.1 Result of the time-lag between physical event and information flow

Week 1	Week 2	Week 3	Week 4	Week 5
Normal output −200	Normal output +200	Normal output −400	Normal output +800	Normal output −1600
	Information received for week 1	Information received for week 2	Information received for week 3	Information received for week 4
	Corrective action +200	Corrective action −400	Corrective action +800	Corrective action −1600
	Adjusted output +400	Adjusted output −800	Adjusted output +1600	Adjusted output −3200

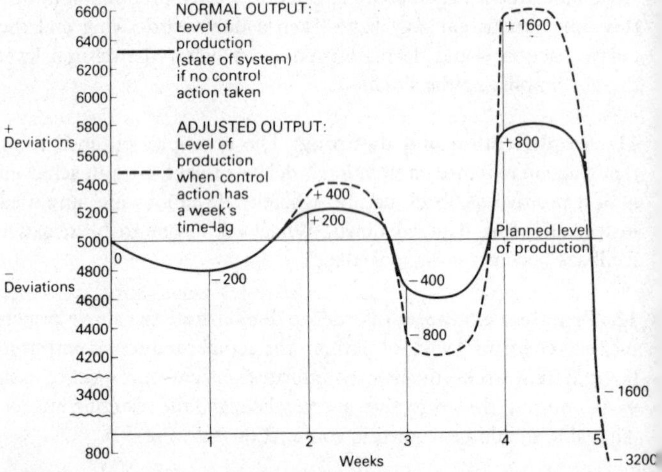

Figure 9.3 *Effect of time-lag in an oscillating system*

of periodical short-term accounting reports, statements and statistics. This involves reporting on events as soon after the conclusion of an operating control period as is feasible, so as to effect adjustments to the situations being controlled, either to eliminate adverse variances or to take advantage of favourable conditions.

It is important to appreciate that the best possible type of information will not effect control without a human or automated controller to effect adjustments to the systems being controlled, based on the information provided. The time factor must be considered with regard to its importance in achieving the degree of control required. For example, if information in respect of scrapped production is not reported early enough, no remedial action can be taken to stop production and to remove the cause of the scrap. It becomes necessary to introduce quality controllers to monitor the quality of production at strategic locations in the production processes. By this means, production may be stopped when it is discovered that the acceptable level of quality is not being achieved. Quality control charts are normally employed for monitoring the quality of production. By this means, corrective action may be taken to remove the cause of the scrap and so ensure that production achieves the desired level of quality (the desired state of the system).

14. Hunting or oscillating. Business activities hardly ever achieve a steady state as they are subjected to random influences from both the internal and the external environments. This causes results, or the level of performance, to fluctuate above and below the average or normal state. For example, stocks of materials attain an overall average level, but vary on day-to-day basis, which is a normal state of affairs. It is extreme variations which must be controlled, as these cause a system to 'hunt' or 'oscillate' around its standard or normal state, corrective action being effected as a result of feedback. The effect of negative and positive feedback in an oscillating system is shown in Figs. 9.4. and 9.5.

15. Buffeting. Unusual disturbances to a system's behaviour are caused by 'buffeting' and this results in fluctuating system states, i.e. a tendency to 'hunt' or 'oscillate' and deviate from the desired course. For example, a strong cross wind on a motorway will buffet a motor vehicle, causing it to deviate sharply from the desired direction. The driver of the vehicle must apply corrective action to remedy the effect of the cross wind, usually by the application of negative feedback, i.e. steering in the opposite direction to the wind. (*See* also **14** and **17**.)

16. System tuning. When a car engine is out of tune it does not run smoothly and is said to be out of tune. To improve its performance it must be retuned, and the same considerations apply to business

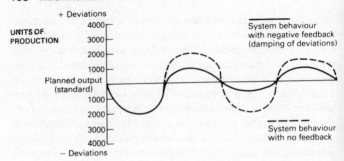

Figure 9.4 *Effect of negative feedback in an oscillating system*

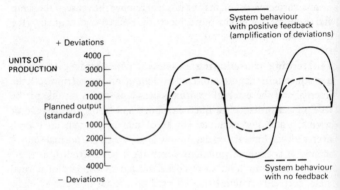

Figure 9.5 *Effect of positive feedback in an oscillating system*

systems as they also require retuning from time to time to accord with current circumstances. This is the reason systems studies take place, to modify the operations performed in a system or the method employed.

17. Homeostasis. Systems, to be effective, must maintain a state of balance, which requires the elimination of unnecessary 'hunting' or 'oscillating'. The term 'homeostasis' may be defined as the process of holding steady or 'balancing' the output of a system, i.e. the 'controlled variable', despite disturbances and 'buffeting'. It is the process of restoring a system to its desired state when subjected to changing environmental conditions (*see* **14** and **15**).

In a stock control system, unusual variations in demand and supply may be interpreted as disturbances to normal behaviour. Safety stocks are integrated into the system to overcome this situation, but in the case of extreme variations the stock control parameters (reference input) may require modification to allow for changing trends.

With regard to a heating system, a thermostat situated in a water tank holds the temperature of the water steady – in a state of balance – because when the heater is switched on the temperature rises to the desired level and the thermostat then switches off the heater. After a while the water temperature begins to fall and when it is below the desired level the thermostat switches the heater back on. This action maintains the system in a steady state.

A further example of homeostasis is outlined in **1** in respect of the Watt governor.

18. Response time. This term is usually used in the context of computing systems and is a measure of the time elapsed from making a request for information to the time it takes for the computer to respond. A clerical information system may react too slowly to requests for information which is one of the reasons why MISs are often computer-oriented. In real-time systems a computer must respond to changing circumstances as they occur in order that the system may be effectively controlled.

Communication theory

Before defining specific aspects of communication and noise in the narrow sense of everyday business activities, it is important to appreciate the wider concepts involved in communication.

All systems contain the element of communication, especially closed-loop systems providing the basis of feedback. Communication may therefore be defined as the provision of information on which a decision to control the state of a system may be based (*see* Fig. 9.1).

19. Elements of communication. The elements of communication may be described by an example from telecommunications; a wireless operator using a morse key transmits messages to a distant location where they are received by another wireless operator who records the messages.

The elements of such activities are as follows.

(*a*) *Information source*. Originator of message wishing to convey information to another person.

(*b*) *Message*. Details of situation on message pad.

(*c*) *Transmitter*. Wireless operator transmitting message by means of morse key connected to transmitting set.

(*d*) *Signal*. The signal produced by the transmitting set when the morse key is depressed.

(*e*) *Receiver*. Wireless operator receiving message by means of a receiving set and earphones and writing message on a message pad.

(*f*) *Information destination*. Receipt of message by addressee.

20. Elements of communication in cost control system. In order to relate the elements of communication outlined above to a business environment, a cost control system is given here as an example: it is desired to communicate the incidence of scrap production to the cost control system.

(*a*) *Information source*. Inspector responsible for informing cost office of scrap production.

(*b*) *Message*. Details of scrap recorded on scrap notes (source documents).

(*c*) *Transmitter*. Distribution of scrap notes by messenger service.

(*d*) *Signal*. Delivery of scrap notes to cost office.

(*e*) *Receiver*. Cost clerk receiving scrap notes.

(*f*) *Information destination*. This may be the cost clerk receiving the scrap notes, or the cost controller after the cost clerk has processed the scrap notes.

21. The noise element in communications. Noise is a telecommunications term which indicates the presence of unwanted signals in electrical and electronic devices. In the context of data communication, noise is any disturbance to the transmission of the required signal which causes the signal being received to differ from the signal transmitted. In the business context, this implies that as the effective control of business is dependent upon accurate information, the incidence of noise is likely to distort the information being received by either the controller or the effector. Consequently the state of a system may be misinterpreted as a result of the distorted information, and incorrect action to remedy the situation may be applied.

In general terms, noise alters the content of a message received from that which is meant to be conveyed. This situation can arise simply by misinterpretation of the context of a message, the use of terms not understood by the recipient (jargon), the presence of static on the line during a telephone conversation, too much padding in a report which tends to hide the essential facts, and inadequately worded communications, etc.

22. Redundancy and the noise factor. The element of redundancy is often incorporated into communications to overcome the problem of noise. Redundancy refers to the addition of bits, characters or digits to ensure that messages are received correctly or that the correct record is being processed. Examples of redundancy are as follows.

(a) The spelling-out of a value in addition to presenting it in the normal way, i.e. £20 (twenty pounds).

(b) The inclusion of a parity bit (binary digit) in addition to the bit combination of a character in coded form. The parity bit is an additional 1 bit which is included in character codes punched into paper tape or encoded on magnetic tape for either data transmission or data transfer in computer operations. The parity bit is inserted automatically by the data preparation equipment, and is for the purpose of checking that data is being transferred or transmitted free of corruption. A 1 bit is added to ensure that the 1 bits accord either to an even number count or to an odd number count, depending on the mode in use.

(c) Quite frequently in computer data processing applications, check digits are used to ensure the accuracy of stock numbers and account numbers prior to processing. A check digit is a number which is added to such numbers for the purpose of producing a 'self-checking' number. A check digit has a unique mathematical relationship to the number to which it is added. The editing routine of a computer program performs check digit verification and data is rejected as invalid when the check digit derived is any number other than the correct one. (*See* 5: **11–15**)

23. Redundancy and management reports. Redundancy incorporated in management reports tends to overshadow the essential facts. For example, a complete listing of cost-centre budgeted and actual expenditure, although conveying all the facts, does not in fact convey a clear appreciation of the situation directly. The manager concerned is required to establish the significance of each of the items listed by going through the list item by item comparing each budgeted and actual expenditure amount to determine those which require his immediate attention.

If reporting is restricted to items with significant variations of actual expenditure from budgeted expenditure, then a greater impact is made and the recipient of the report can speedily respond to the situation disclosed. In the complete listing indicated above, the significant details were not highlighted and in fact the essential requirement, the disclosure of variances, was not included. In such a case, the control system is inefficient, as a complete listing in such a case is an obstacle to the clear understanding of the situation.

Progress test 9

1. A company operates a stock control procedure which has the essential features of a closed-loop system, comprising: (*a*) stores, dealing with the physical receipt, holding and issue of materials; (*b*) a stock control office which: (*i*) is supplied with copies of goods received notes, requisitions and return to store notes; (*ii*) maintains stock records; (*iii*) establishes parameters for stock and re-order levels, incorporating future usage data from the production control department; (*iv*) originates purchase requisition as required; (*c*) a purchasing department.

You are required to draw an outline flowchart of the system described, showing the necessary major information flows and linkages. Identify on your chart the three points in the system which function as sensor, comparator and effector. (Figure 9.2 may be used as the basis for the solution.) (*CIMA*)

2. Define the nature of feedback. (**1**)

3. Define and discuss the characteristics of negative and positive feedback in relation to information systems. Give an example of each. (**2, 3**) (*CIMA*)

4. Define the term 'feedforward'. (**4**)

5. Define the nature of 'open-loop' and 'closed-loop' systems. (**5–9**)

6. Using a computerised inventory control system as background: (a) explain what is meant by 'automatic decision-making'; (b) state the factors which should be taken into account when a systems designer is considering whether or not to incorporate this feature; (c) state the safeguards which should be included in the system if automatic decision-making is incorporated. (**7, 8**) (*CIMA*)

7. The quality of management information is directly related to its timing. (a) Discuss this statement, with particular reference to: (i) the different purposes for which the information may be required; and (ii) the relative merits of speed versus accuracy in each case. (b) Explain in what ways the timing of information flows should be taken into account when designing information systems. (**10–13, 18**) (*CIMA*)

8. Explain the following system terms: (a) hunting or oscillating; (b) buffeting; (c) system tuning; (d) homeostasis; (e) response time. (**14–18**)

9. Indicate the basic elements of communication both in telecommunications and the normal business environment. (**19, 20**)

10. Define what is meant by 'noise' in communications. (**21**)

11. 'Redundancy is very often incorporated into business communications to overcome the problem of noise but can on occasions create noise.' Discuss this statement. (**22, 23**)

Part five
Systems design

10
Principles of systems design

Initial considerations

1. The need for systems development. A system designed for one set of circumstances will not be compatible with the needs of a different set of circumstances. The dynamic nature of a business requires the implementation of change to contend with the factors influencing its activities. The present is a time of intense technological development, and it is often necessary to harness the latest technology available to the functions and activities of a business to enable it to become or remain administratively efficient in comparison with its competitors. Change is often forced upon a business because competitors develop their systems for greater productivity or efficiency, or as a result of business take-overs when it may be necessary to reappraise the administrative systems in use in order to standardise them or to remove or replace those which are outmoded.

2. Steering committee. The implementation of new technology needs to be planned within the corporate framework as a whole, rather than haphazardly on the wishes of individual managers. Dysfunctional effects will otherwise be incurred because of fragmented and unco-ordinated projects. It is the responsibility of a steering committee to assess the viability of computer projects. It must ensure that such projects are cost-effective and create benefits to the business as a whole rather than merely to individual functions which can result in imbalances and give rise to sub-optimal results.

Membership of the committee should be representative of the organisation and should consist of personnel from the various functions which will be affected by future computerisation of systems. The interests of functions can then be considered as a whole and it is possible to assess whether proposals will be compatible with the future strategy of the business.

3. Application of new technology. New technology in the form of computers and related electronic systems such as on-line information processing systems, electronic mail and local area networks, etc., should eliminate existing weaknesses within the organisation or function. Such weaknesses are often due to outmoded practices and worn out machines and equipment incompatible with current needs. When weaknesses are eliminated the more a business is in a position to meet new challenges or to increase productivity. It will be able to reduce operating costs and increase the rate of output of information as well as streamline operations to increase administrative efficiency. It is by responding to 'change' that businesses 're-arm' to meet the challenges offered to them by the environment.

Changing from predominantly manual or mechanically oriented systems to sophisticated electronic systems creates fundamental changes to the nature of resources used. Manpower in particular tends to be replaced by machine power. It is important to appreciate, however, that the most highly developed and sophisticated systems need an element of manual supportive activities.

4. Problem analysis. Before it is possible to develop computerised versions of existing systems it is necessary to identify the fundamental problem(s) which exist in the current system. It is pointless attempting to develop a new system if the problems existing in the current one remain unidentified. It is important to appreciate that that which, on the surface, appears to be the problem may not be the problem itself but the result of having the problem.

For example, a system may seem to have a bottleneck in the processing of forms and it is thought that a computerised system will speed up the flow of work and so remove the problem. If, however, the underlying cause of the bottleneck is the processing of either obsolete documents or obsolete details on current documents, then the system merely requires restructuring by eliminating the 'dead wood'. Converting the system would not only incur system development costs but also would not solve the problem since it is not one of processing but a result of a failure to eliminate obsolescence.

5. Key factors for the selection of projects. Projects for development may be selected on the basis of 'key factors' which indicate areas of improvement and therefore the greatest potential for achieving the greatest benefits. Large cost savings on a low cost activity do not generate the required magnitude of benefits as a reduction of 50 per cent on operating costs of £5000 is only £2500 but a 10 per cent reduction on operating costs of £150,000 is a saving of £15,000 which is of greater relative significance.

Key factors for consideration include those listed below:

(a) systems with a high volume of errors;
(b) systems with a high volume of output;
(c) systems with a large number of operations;
(d) systems with a large number of personnel;
(e) systems with high operating costs;
(f) systems suffering from bottlenecks causing delays in the distribution of information for business control;
(g) systems functioning with outdated methods;
(h) systems which do not accord with current needs;
(i) systems which are too complicated for their primary purpose.

Systems competing for scarce development resources

6. Strategy. What strategy should be adopted when several systems are being considered for computerisation and there is a shortage of systems development staff? This is the theme of a question set by the Chartered Association of Certified Accountants in their December 1985 Systems Analysis and Design paper and is outlined below. A suggested solution follows in **7–9.**

'There are several manual procedures which are being considered for transfer to a computer in the organisation for which you work. There is, however, a shortage of systems development staff, so only one of the proposed systems can be approved for development at this stage.

Required:
(a) Briefly describe *five* factors which you would use in selecting the one system to be developed.
(b) Identify *five* possible courses of action which may be taken to overcome the shortage of systems development staff and thus permit the more rapid implementation of the systems.'

7. Basis for selection. Before it is possible to draw positive conclusions from a diverse list of factors as a basis for selection it is advisable to prepare a summary of factors which could be used in selecting the one system to be developed. These are indicated below:

(*a*) Prepare a list of the important factors which will provide a basis for selecting one system for development.

(*b*) Award points to each factor of each system from a maximum of ten for the purpose of indicating the relative weighting (importance) of the individual factors.

(*c*) Select the system with the highest points rating (score) for development.

8. List of factors. The factors to include in the list are:

(*a*) *Cost effectiveness.* If staff savings are a necessity then the system that reduces the staff by the greatest number will score the highest number of points. Alternatively, the system which avoids increasing staff numbers by the highest number will score most points. An additional factor would be based on the reduction of total operating costs.

(*b*) *Operational efficiency.* The system which, if computerised, will achieve the highest level of operational efficiency will be the favourite contender. This may be assessed in terms of the number of days saved at the month-end to produce statements of account, or the staff payroll, or month-end accounts. An additional factor could be based on the relative importance of achieving a greater degree of accuracy in the preparation of invoices for instance. This has a bearing on customer satisfaction and the creation of a greater degree of goodwill. If the stock control system is a contender then it may be assessed on the value of the reduced level of stocks which will be possible due to improved stock management and control.

(*c*) *Development time and relative use of resources.* If time is of the essence to implement a computerised system then the system which will take the shortest time will score best. Alternatively, or in addition to the time factor, the system which utilises the lowest level of systems resources by way of systems analysts' time will score most points.

(*d*) *Simplicity.* The system which is the simplest to install may be looked upon in a favourable light as a system with few complications (if there is such a thing) will achieve results as outlined in (*c*) above.

(e) *Company image*. The installation of a particular type of system may be a prestigious achievement for a company and may have a spin-off by way of an increase in the level of goodwill. This may apply to an automated purchase order system which provides suppliers with a forward supply schedule and which provides for prompt payment of supplies.

(f) *Improved flow of management information*. Businesses must be controlled effectively to remain efficient or even to survive. A system which improves managerial performance by the provision of more timely information will tend to score well.

(g) *Improved problem-solving and decision-making*. Any system which will provide management with facts on which timely decisions may be based or which provides the means of solving important strategic or tactical problems will tend to be favourably considered.

9. Overcoming shortages of systems development staff. Five possible courses of action to overcome the shortage of systems development staff and permit the more rapid implementation of systems include:

(a) Employ a systems house to develop the systems.

(b) Use program generators (*see* 19: **19–22**).

(c) Use application packages (*see* 19: **3–8**).

(d) Employ freelance systems and programming personnel (from advertisements in computer journals and magazines).

(e) Enlist the services of a recruitment agency to obtain trained staff.

(f) Employ the services of a personnel agency for the hiring of temporary staff (similar to (d) above).

(g) Employ a training organisation for training suitable personnel on a short-duration external or in-plant course.

(Two additional courses of action have been added to the number required by the question.)

Design factors, criteria and constraints

10. List of factors. A number of important factors must be considered when designing information systems to achieve cost and operational effectiveness. Some of these are outlined below.

(a) Information must be produced at the right time, at the right cost, in the right format, at the right level of accuracy and by the right media.

(b) Routine decisions should be automated, e.g. those relating to the automatic ordering of stock.

(c) Source data should be prepared in the most suitable manner.

(d) The system under review should not be considered in isolation from other sub-systems (*see* 3: **5–6**).

(e) A system should be designed within the context of the requirements of the business as a whole, i.e. within the corporate framework, even though it is confined to a specific sub-system initially.

(f) Sub-systems should be designed with future integration with other sub-systems in mind.

(g) Checks and controls should be incorporated which are capable of detecting and reporting errors.

(h) Suitable coding systems should be incorporated for effective reference, comparison, sorting and validation.

(i) Computer runs should be efficiently structured.

(j) Effective safeguards should be incorporated for the prevention of fraud and for privacy and confidentiality.

(k) The time and cost of encoding data from source documents should be minimised.

(l) The direct input of source data should be considered in the context of on-line systems.

(m) Data should always be processed as efficiently as possible avoiding unnecessary complexity.

(n) File security measures must be adequate.

(o) Fail-safe and restart procedures should be incorporated as appropriate.

(p) Business policy matters should be incorporated in so far as they are relevant to a specific system.

(q) Relevant legislation should be provided for.

(r) Exception routines should be catered for.

(s) Screen layouts should be clear and unambiguous.

(t) Parameters should be clearly defined.

(u) Specific attention should be accorded to the effective design of supporting clerical systems as well as computer operations.

(v) Systems should be as simple as possible keeping in view the requirements of the operating department staff, i.e. the users.

(*w*) Dialogue design should not be overcomplicated to facilitate ease of understanding by the work station/terminal operators.

(*x*) All forms should be designed for utmost simplicity of use.

(*y*) Systems documentation should be complete and standardised.

(*z*) The utmost co-operation and co-ordination is essential between all interested parties.

11. Design criteria and constraints. Apart from having to meet system objectives the systems analyst needs to establish criteria for the design process and be fully aware of constraints to any proposed strategy. A number of such factors will now be considered.

(*a*) *Portability*. Portability means that programs written for one machine can be run on another without modification. This requires the formulation of a specific migration path keeping to one manufacturer to avoid reprogramming or, at least, recompiling, as would be necessary if switching to a different manufacturer.

(*b*) *Integrity*. This is the attainment of a specified level of service together with the desired level of system availability and the accomplishment of the required degree of privacy, confidentiality, accuracy, security and reliability of data.

(*c*) *Efficiency of system performance*. This refers to matters relating to minimising computer run time and optimising system response times for critical on-line applications.

(*d*) *Integration*. The combination of separately structured systems to form a larger streamlined fully automated system in the quest for a 'total system'.

(*e*) *Project life constraints*. Minimising the time and resources utilised on the project, perhaps because of a scarcity of system development resources for competing projects.

(*f*) *Financial constraints*. The projected costs of a project's development must be related to anticipated benefits to ensure it is an economically viable proposition.

(*g*) *Simplicity of design and user-friendliness*. Systems must always be designed with simplicity and user-friendliness in mind, remembering that system design is a means to an end and not an end in itself.

(*h*) *Standardisation*. Design standards should be considered, but not at the expense of rigidity and inflexibility.

The approach to systems design

12. Summary of approaches. There are many different approaches which may be adopted for designing business systems, but no single approach may be used as it may be more effective to use a combination, e.g. a modular and total system approach. These include:

(a) input-to-output approach;
(b) output-to-input approach;
(c) top-down approach;
(d) bottom-up approach;
(e) total system approach;
(f) piecemeal (functional) systems approach;
(g) modular systems approach;
(h) data-driven approach;
(i) problem-driven approach;
(j) process-driven approach;
(k) database approach;
(l) logical (structured) approach.

Each of these approaches will now be outlined.

13. Input-to-output approach. This approach first considers the input to the system and then assesses what processing operations are needed to convert the data to specific output. Emphasis is on the input element of the system, i.e. the transaction data. This approach requires a careful assessment of the data that is needed to produce the desired output. The system will otherwise produce output from existing data rather than that which is required. This is the only way in which useful reports can be produced which fully serve the needs of management and administration.

14. Output-to-input approach. This is the opposite approach to the stance adopted by the input-to-output approach. Emphasis is rightly placed upon the output requirements of the system (remember that output is the end product of an information processing system). With this approach it is necessary to determine the required content of the reports and documents and so establish the data flows required to produce them. It may be necessary to eliminate some data flows or data fields and originate new or modified fields to ensure data is compatible with current rather than historical needs.

15. Top-down approach. This approach initially considers management strategic needs and goals prior to specifying operational data requirements. The higher level functions are then progressively analysed into more detail, a process known as 'functional decomposition'. It may be necessary to review the impact of lower level situations or operational needs on the higher level functions in order to determine whether it is necessary to revise the higher level goals.

16. Bottom-up approach. This approach is probably the most widely adopted in conjunction with the output-to-input approach. Logically, the system is designed from scratch, starting with the basic operational needs of the system and specifying the input documents and output requirements to deal with routine administrative needs. It is then built up, rather in the way a house is built up on its foundations, to the higher level requirements by adding data analysis and exception reporting routines as the basis of a management information system. This approach not only provides for the operational level but also provides information for managerial decision-making and strategic planning.

17. Total system approach. The 'total' system approach requires a detailed analysis of all the business systems to identify the relationships which exist between them. This may relate to intercommunications and data flows which act as interfaces between the various sub-systems. It is important to be aware of the effect on a system of the behaviour of a related system.

18. Piecemeal (functional) systems approach. This approach to systems design has a tendency to generate sub-optimisation as systems are developed in isolation from each other. The approach considers only the needs of specific functions, and not how functions may interact.

19. Modular approach. A complex system may be analysed into a series of related sub-systems, each sub-system being a 'module' of the overall system. The approach achieves flexibility as a number of modules can be developed concurrently. Program debugging, testing and maintenance is facilitated by this approach. Modules may also be designed so that in the event of one module failing the others can continue functioning. This is known as 'graceful degradation'.

20. Data-driven approach. The philosophy behind this approach is that the approach to systems design should be related to the structure of the data to be processed rather than the processes to be performed. If the design of the system is related to the output generated by the data then it can be classed as a 'data flow' approach. If, however, the approach relates to the storage and organisation of data it is 'a data structure' driven approach.

21. Problem-driven approach. This approach commences by identifying the problems inherent in the current system. The problems are then resolved before proceeding with other elements of the system.

22. Process-driven approach. This approach views the system as a series of functions, i.e. the tasks which need to be done, rather than the inputs and outputs from the system. This may be defined as a 'system designer' approach rather than a 'user' approach.

23. Database approach. This approach requires the analysis of the data relating to the system being designed for incorporation into a database to be controlled by a database management system (DBMS). As systems design progresses to other systems, the data already in the database may be suitable for their use, thereby avoiding the need to duplicate common data in other files. This is what occurs if functional files are developed rather than a consolidated collection of data providing for the needs of various functions.

24. Logical (structured) approach. This approach creates a detailed description of a new system without considering hardware, software or other physical requirements. The logical system is designed on the basis of system objectives. (*See* also **16** above and 14: **19–27**.)

Progress test 10

1. Why is it necessary to implement 'change' to business systems? (**1**)

2. What is the nature, purpose and composition of a steering committee? (**2**)

3. New technology should eliminate existing weaknesses in a business. Discuss. (**3**)

4. Before it is possible to develop computerised versions of existing systems it is necessary to identify the problems which exist in the current system. Discuss. (**4**)

5. Projects for development may be selected on the basis of 'key factors'. List a number of such factors. (**5**)

6. Outline the strategy which could be adopted when several systems are competing for computerisation and a shortage of systems development staff exists. (**6–8**)

7. How may the shortage of systems development staff be overcome? (**9**)

8. A number of factors must be considered when designing information systems to achieve cost and operational effectiveness. List several such factors. (**10**)

9. What criteria and constraints should be kept in mind by a system designer when developing computerised systems. (**11**)

10. There are many different approaches which may be adopted for designing business systems, four of which are:

(*a*) input-to-output,
(*b*) top-down,
(*c*) modular,
(*d*) problem-driven.

Outline the main features of each of these approaches. (**12, 13, 15, 19, 21**)

11
Important factors relating to systems design

Terms of reference

1. Authority for conducting an assignment. Terms of reference constitute the authority to systems development staff to undertake a feasibility study of a system(s). They should preferably be in writing to avoid any misinterpretation or ambiguity at a later date.

Typical contents of the terms of reference include:

(a) boundaries to the assignment;
(b) purpose and objectives of the system under consideration;
(c) priority rating of the project.

2. Boundaries to the assignment. It is important for the boundaries of an assignment to be clearly defined otherwise investigations can be needlessly pursued into the domain of other systems. It is a simple matter to 'stray' into an adjoining operational area because of the close relationships which exist between many sub-systems. If, for instance, the boundary is stipulated as being the 'stock control system' then it should not overspill into the related area of the purchasing system, even though they are very closely related.

3. Purpose and objectives. The purpose and objectives of the system(s) to be investigated must be stated at the outset otherwise the project would have no defined aims. For example, the purpose of a stock control system may be defined as: 'To record details of stock movements (i.e. stock transactions) on stock records for the purpose of being aware of the latest status of each item in the stores for stock management requirements.' In addition, the objectives may be defined as: 'To control the level of stocks by means of stock control parameters (i.e minimum, maximum and recorder levels) to avoid frequent stock shortages and to minimise stock levels and the cost of carrying stocks (storage costs) as a basis for achieving stock optimisation.'

4. Priority rating of project. The priority rating of the project must be clearly specified in relation to the other projects which are concurrently under review. This avoids any doubt in the mind of investigators of the course of action to pursue at any point in time as a result of manpower absences or similar problems. Personnel may then be deployed as the situation dictates with impunity.

5. Modifying terms of reference. As investigations proceed the initial terms of reference may require modification, either to eliminate an element of ambiguity, to incorporate new factors previously overlooked or to revise the boundary of a project to integrate several related sub-systems, e.g. order processing, despatching, invoicing, sales ledger and stock control.

Feasibility study

6. Nature of a feasibility study. In the context of computers used in business for information processing systems a feasibility study may be defined as a preliminary survey of the business environment. Its purpose is to establish if a business would benefit either from implementing a computer for business systems as a whole, from computerising a specific business system, or from upgrading an existing system.

7. Management decision. Management are required to make a decision whether to implement a computer or to computerise a specific system on the basis of a feasibility study report. The correct decision is crucial, particularly if a mainframe or minicomputer is under consideration, because of the cost of the resources employed in developing systems if a decision is made to go ahead. The gains can be quite substantial, as indicated by the summary of benefits in 18: **8–9** but the losses can also be quite high if the wrong decision is made.

If management make a decision not to implement a computer when one should be implemented, an improvement in administrative and operational efficiency compared to that of competitors will be forgone. On the other hand, the consequence of implementing a large computer when one is not needed is administrative chaos because current systems will be disrupted needlessly due to system development activities; the systems subsequently implemented may not operate smoothly and fail to achieve objectives because they were invalid initially but failed to be assessed as such because of inadequate investigations.

The success of any computerised system will depend upon the extent of the attention to detail applied when assessing the inherent problems of the current systems and the objectives to be achieved. It is therefore essential to discuss problem areas with relevant managers and operations staff, examine the forms and documents processed, the machines and equipment in use, the calibre of staff engaged on the various activities, policy matters relating to such aspects as discount rates in relation to value of sales orders, delivery charges in relation to value of orders and delivery distance, credit policy in relation to specific classes of customer, and so on.

8. Feasibility study report. A feasibility study report may typically consist of four main sections, comprising hardware and software, staffing, operating costs and expected benefits. Areas for consideration under each of these topics are outlined below.

(*a*) *Hardware and software*:

(*i*) Alternative types of computer configuration available which must be considered when initially assessing the use of a computer.

(*ii*) The need for standby facilities in case of breakdown of the in-house computer.

(*iii*) Information processing trends and their likely effect on the type and size of computer required.

(*iv*) Availability of software packages for the systems under consideration.

(*v*) Additional hardware/software requirements for proposed systems.

Items (*i*) to (*iv*) are relevant to the initial implementation of a computer in a business; items (*iv*) and (*v*) are relevant when considering the computerisation of proposed systems on an existing computer configuration.

(b) Staffing:

(*i*) The availability of experienced computer personnel for staffing the new computer.

(*ii*) Incidence of redundancy of existing clerical personnel.

(*iii*) Need for computer appreciation courses for management and staff.

(*iv*) Need for retraining existing personnel to suit the needs of the computerised systems.

(*v*) Extent to which the organisation will need restructuring when systems are transferred to the computer. Some sections will be phased out, others will be depleted in numbers, a new computer department will come into existence and other sections of the organisation will be merged.

Items (*i*)–(*v*) are particularly relevant on the initial installation of a computer, but items (*ii*)–(*iv*) and some aspects of (*v*) also apply when transferring systems to an existing computer.

(c) Operating costs – *see* 18: **5**.

(d) Expected benefits – *see* 18: **8–9**.

Each system run on the computer would be expected to carry a fair share of all costs incurred in operating the information processing (data processing) department as it provides a service to all participating functions. Such functions, by having data processed for them, are not incurring the cost of the processing resources directly but are using the resources of the servicing department.

9. Personnel involved with the feasibility study. The number and type of personnel required to perform the feasibility study depends upon the circumstances. If the study is in order to establish whether a large computer should be installed into the organisation, then it would be carried out by systems analysts or O & M staff. If systems analysts were not employed in the organisation at this time then it may be necessary to enlist the services of a computer consultancy. However, if O & M staff are already employed, then they may be utilised for the study because of their intimate knowledge of business systems. They often become the new systems analysts in the organisation.

In any event it is advisable to co-opt the services of personnel of the operating departments involved with the investigation, whether it is for the initial implementation of a computer or the transfer of a system to the existing computer. The reason for this strategy is that they have a detailed working knowledge of the relevant systems and are fully conversant with their strengths and weaknesses. This is invaluable information for the design of a successful computerised system. If stock control is under consideration then a member of that department should participate in the study. Similarly, a member of the accounting department should join the team if accounting systems are under investigation.

Stages of systems design

10. System life-cycle. The stages of system life-cycle development are summarised below. A number of the stages are dealt with in greater depth elsewhere, particularly those relating to feasibility study, terms of reference, and systems analysis and design. The stages are as follows.

(a) Define the problem.
(b) Management specify terms of reference (*see* **1–5**).
(c) Conduct feasibility study (*see* **6–9**):
   (i) Technical feasibility: demands on the system regarding terminal enquiries or volume of data to be processed by batch or on-line processing; speed of system response required and the capability of hardware and software to meet these requirements.
   (ii) Economic feasibility: matters relating to cost/benefit appraisal.
(d) Present report to management with recommendations.
(e) Plan the project.
(f) Carry out systems analysis:
   (i) fact-finding (collecting the facts including environment and functional analysis);
   (ii) verify the facts;
   (iii) record the facts;
   (iv) procedure analysis.
(g) System design:
   (i) Design philosophy:
      (1) establish design objectives and constraints;

(2) design alternative systems.

(*ii*)　Design activities:

(1) prepare procedure charts (for clerical activities) block diagrams and system flowcharts;

(2) determine actions to be taken in respect of specified conditions by means of decision tables;

(3) design input documents and output documents and reports;

(4) design file structures and layout;

(5) develop the structure of computer runs by means of run charts;

(6) evaluate run times;

(7) design screen layouts for on-line terminal operations;

(8) develop dialogue to be used by terminal/work station operators;

(9) develop fail-safe and restart procedures;

(10) develop procedures for file security;

(11) discuss with auditors and develop checks and controls to be incorporated.

(*h*)　Prepare system specification (system definition):

(*i*)　details of the system including clerical and computer procedures, block diagrams, system flowcharts, decision tables and a narrative providing a general description of the system;

(*ii*)　input, output and file specifications and layouts;

(*iii*)　schedule of equipment required by the system including new equipment needs and alternative equipment proposals;

(*iv*)　nature and use of passwords (*see* 14: **17–18**).

(*i*)　Present alternative proposals to management.

(*j*)　Discuss proposals with management.

(*k*)　Management decision – choice of proposals if relevant.

(*l*)　Prepare program specification: statement of program requirements including initialisation, parameters, processing stages, input and output requirements, test data and testing procedure to be applied, checks and controls to be incorporated, exception routines, conditions and actions to be provided for and arrangements for test runs.

(*m*)　Programming (*see* 19: **19–22**):

(*i*)　program procedure charts (flowcharts);

(*ii*)　program coding sheets;

(*iii*)　prepare test data and testing procedures;

(*iv*) prepare validation checks and other controls to be incorporated into the system;

(*v*) compile source programs;

(*vi*) debug programs.

(*n*) Convert files.

(*o*) System testing:

(*i*) prepare precalculated results;

(*ii*) test programs with test data by dry runs, i.e. desk checking;

(*iii*) compare results with precalculated results;

(*iv*) report to management and discuss the results obtained from system testing; decide on future course of action;

(*v*) make appropriate modifications to system or programs and recompile as necessary.

(*p*) Implementation:

(*i*) plan system implementation;

(*ii*) carry out parallel running of old and new system; implement direct change-over or pilot scheme as appropriate;

(*iii*) prepare manuals for supporting department (users) and operation departments, including data preparation and data control clerks.

(*q*) Evaluate results with expectations:

(*i*) monitor system performance in co-ordination with user department;

(*ii*) report to management to discuss the situation and decide on appropriate action;

(*iii*) make relevant adjustments to the system.

(*r*) Maintain system:

(*i*) develop, test and implement improvements;

(*ii*) modify system to accord with changing circumstances;

(*iii*) integrate related systems to improve processing efficiency.

It is important to appreciate that the 'system life-cycle' approach to systems design and development is the traditional approach, but there are now a number of structured analysis and design methodologies currently available. One such methodology is that available from Michael Jackson Systems Limited, who have expanded their structured programming philosophy into the realms of structured systems design (*see* 14: **19**).

Project management and control

11. Analysis of project elements. A project should initially be analysed into primary activities so that the most suitable systems staff may be assigned to their investigation. Staff may be assigned to organisation or communication studies, forms, work flows, data flows, processing operations, file structures and system outputs. In other instances individual systems personnel may be assigned to investigate the whole of a system depending upon the complexity of the project and the available manpower resources.

12. Project life-cycle. The next requirement of project planning is to formulate the project life-cycle by defining the project start date. It is then necessary to estimate the duration time of each constituent component of the initial systems analysis stage. Time for developing a number of alternative proposals will also be required. Time estimates will also be required for writing, compiling and testing programs, systems implementation, the evaluation of results and system maintenance.

It is then possible to assess the prospective completion date of the project. The target time is always difficult to achieve because of the many uncertainties involved, such as problems which are difficult to resolve; elements of a procedure previously not considered as they were not included in the procedure manual or were not apparent but which are found to be critical to the effective operation of the system; unplanned staff absences; and so on. It is, however, important to have a time schedule and a list of essential activities to be performed so that resources may be deployed from lower priority projects when necessary in an attempt to achieve the stated completion time. Any plan is better than no plan at all.

Account must be taken of the sequence in which tasks must be performed. Some activities are dependent upon the completion of others, e.g. it is not possible to write programs until the design of the system is finalised. In other instances various tasks can be performed concurrently, e.g. one investigator can study the organisation and communication structure of a system whilst others are looking into the forms, files and data flows, etc.

13. Planning techniques. Techniques which can be applied for project planning include the use of bar charts (known as Gantt charts) on which the various activities are listed in the form of a schedule. The length of a bar signifies the amount of time allocated to an activity. A more sophisticated technique is the network analysis chart which is useful for specifying the critical path. This consists of those activities which form the longest route through the network. If delays occur on the critical path then the project completion time will be delayed. It is this type of control information which provides the basis for project control as it makes clear when resources need to be deployed to critical activities which are falling behind schedule. In addition, use of structured techniques should assist project planning as it introduces more identifiable checkpoints (*See* 2: **3**).

14. Structure of projects. A project may be structured in a number of ways depending on the scope and complexity of the system under review. A small project may be dealt with through all the constituent stages of analysis and design and perhaps programming, testing and implementation by one all-round systems and programming expert. This of course presupposes that the systems personnel possess a wide range of experience embracing the analysis of current systems and the design of inputs, records, files and outputs for proposed systems including knowledge of processing and data capture techniques, etc.

15. Complex projects. Large complex projects covering a major business function – such as when changing over from manual operations in an accounting department to a fully integrated computerised accounting system – will need to be separated into easily manageable modules consisting of sub-projects each of which is delegated to a project team under the control of a team leader. Each team leader would report to the project co-ordinator. The co-ordinator would take the necessary steps to ensure that all sub-projects were co-ordinated with overall system objectives and reallocate resources in emergencies to compensate for time lost at any stage of the project.

16. Pilot project. A project may consist of developing a pilot project in one section or operating unit of the business, such as a branch of a building society or a branch works. The results obtained from running the pilot system assist in evaluating its suitability for implementation in other locations in the business.

Progress test 11

1. Terms of reference constitute the authority to undertake systems investigations. Indicate the typical contents of formal written terms of reference. (**1–4**)

2. It may be necessary during investigations to modify initial terms of reference. What are the circumstances that would indicate this situation? (**5**)

3. What is the nature and purpose of a feasibility study? (**6, 7**)

4. What main sections should a feasibility study report contain? (**8**)

5. What type of personnel are involved with a feasibility study? (**9**)

6. List the stages of the systems life-cycle. (**10**)

7. How would you manage and control project development activities? (**11–16**)

12
Systems analysis

Principles of systems analysis

1. Characteristics of systems. Systems analysis provides details of the nature, characteristics, problems and weaknesses of a system to be used as a basis for designing a more effective computerised system. Systems analysis requires the co-ordination and co-operation of both specialist systems staff and the personnel of the department concerned with the system investigation, i.e. the user department personnel. Such personnel are seconded to the investigation so that they may participate in the analysis and subsequent design of the system of which they are an integral element.

2. Systems analysis team. Some projects may require a team of investigators depending upon the complexity of the system under review. This topic is discussed in more detail in 11: **11–16**.

Fact-finding

3. Collect the facts. The fact collecting stage of an assignment is extremely important as it enables the systems staff to become familiar with the characteristics and features of the system under review. This is essential before it is possible to design a computerised version of the system. The specific facts to be collected depend upon the nature of the system and the terms of reference, but generally they will include details relating to the following matters:

(*a*) *Resources used*. Details must be collected relating to the number of personnel engaged on the various tasks, the number and type of machines in use for specific operations, the number and types of forms and stationery used and other operating supplies, the use made of computer bureaux, services provided by other departments and so on.

(b) *Operational data*. This data relates to the nature and volume of the various tasks and activities performed, the time taken to perform them and their volume and frequency. It also includes details of bottlenecks and delays in the system as well as other system strengths and weaknesses.

(c) *Operating costs*. This data relates to the costs of running the system in respect of the resources used as indicated in (a) above. Such costs include salaries of staff, supervisors and management; the cost of electricity for heating and the supply of power to machines; machine and building maintenance and insurance costs; operating supplies, i.e. forms and stationery; inter-department service costs and computer bureau charges; depreciation of machines and buildings, etc.

(d) *Organisational data*. This type of data relates to the number of personnel engaged on each activity, their job titles, superior/subordinate relationships and the span of control of the various supervisors.

(e) *Communication analysis*. It is often necessary to establish the lines of communication which exist within a system, i.e. the incidence of intercommunications between personnel in the same department, within a section and between other sub-systems and functions of the organisation. This is indicative of the nature of the communications which will be required by the proposed computer system. This may include the need for on-line terminals, electronic mail, access to a database, distributed processing for intercommunication between computers and random enquiry facilities, etc.

(f) *Company policy matters*. It is essential to be aware of the various policies which exist and the manner in which they relate to the various systems. In respect of personnel policy, for example, this would embrace matters relating to long-service increments which must be provided for in the payroll system; in respect of the sales system this would embrace matters relating to the level of discounts in relation to sales values, the credit limit and credit period allowed to specified customers and the policy in respect of delivery charges in relation to value of sales; and so on.

(g) *Data analysis*. Establishing the nature of the data used in the business, the users and its purpose.

Fact-finding techniques

4. Primary questions. Any person concerned with fact-finding, whether for normal work simplification or with a view to computerising a system, must apply a methodical approach to ensure important facts are not overlooked. To this end a pre-prepared checklist may be used containing the main points to which answers are essential. The checklist is based on a framework of fundamental questions which are:

(a) *What* is done?
(b) *Why* is it done?
(c) *When* is it done?
(d) *How* is it done?
(e) *Where* is it done?
(f) *Who* does it?

If the answer to the question, 'Why is it done?' indicates that the system provides a useful purpose, the fundamental questions outlined above may be expanded as follows:

(a) Purpose: *What* is done? This requires a definition of the activities performed which may be, for instance, the calculation of wages based on the hours worked by employees as recorded on time cards.

(b) Means: *How* is it done? Details are required of the resources and methods used to accomplish the defined activities, including:

(i)   forms used;
(ii) machines and equipment used;
(iii) method/technique used, e.g. three-in-one posting method using a writing board whereby three related documents are posted simultaneously.

(c) Personnel: *Who* does it? Details of the personnel performing the activities are required which may include:

(i)   the number of personnel engaged on the activity both full-time and part-time;
(ii) job titles and the skills required;
(iii) type of staff – male or female.

(d) Location: *Where* is it done? The details required in this instance relate to the place where the activity is performed as follows:

(i)   which factory, branch office or site;
(ii) function;
(iii) department;

(*iv*) section.

(*e*) Time/sequence: *When* is it done? Details of the time period and the sequence in which the activity is performed are required on the basis of the following details:

(*i*) day, week, month;
(*ii*) sequence – before activity *x*;
(*iii*) sequence – after activity *y*.

After completing the checklist based on the questions outlined above, it will be necessary to test the validity of the responses.

5. Methods of collecting facts. In addition to using the checklist approach a number of other methods of collecting facts may be used including:

(*a*) interviewing;
(*b*) observation;
(*c*) questionnaire;
(*d*) inspection.

See Volume 1 for further details of these methods.

Recording the facts

6. Advantages of recording facts. The systems analyst may record details of procedures on procedure charts to provide a pictorial representation of each procedure. This is normally done at the recording stage of system development when all the facts are assembled into some semblance of order. At this point the facts may be further verified by requesting the operating staff to check the charts for completeness, absence of duplication and any inaccuracies.

The verification of facts provides a number of important advantages including:

(*a*) establishes the reliability of facts;
(*b*) indicates omissions;
(*c*) eliminates ambiguity;
(*d*) avoids duplication of activities;
(*e*) elicits valuable suggestions from operating personnel;
(*f*) highlights matters for further investigation;
(*g*) increases the effectiveness of proposed systems.

7. Recording techniques. Having collected the relevant facts on the current system it is necessary to organise them into a form which can be fully understood and critically examined prior to the design of a computerised version. A number of recording techniques can be used depending on the type of facts to be recorded. These include:

(*a*) procedure charts;
(*b*) procedure narratives;
(*c*) procedure maps;
(*d*) organisation charts.

Progress test 12

1. Systems analysis is a fact-finding activity. State the primary purpose of fact-finding. (**1**)

2. Fact-finding requires the collection of facts of different categories. Define the nature of several categories. (**3**)

3. Fact – finding requires the asking of primary questions. Define the nature of such questions. (**4**)

4. Name four methods of collecting facts. (**5**)

5. Facts collected during systems analysis need to be recorded. What are the advantages of recording facts? (**6**)

6. Facts may be recorded using a number of techniques. Specify four such techniques. (**7**)

13
Recording and communicating techniques

1. Summary of recording techniques. In order to compare and contrast decision tables and flowcharts in systems design the following definitions are provided in subsequent paragraphs:

(a) flowcharting;
(b) flowchart symbols;
(c) block diagram;
(d) system flowchart;
(e) computer runchart (*see* 19: **19–22**);
(f) data flow diagram;
(g) system structure chart;
(h) decision table.

Flowcharts

2. Flowcharting. A technique adopted by system designers for representing the features and characteristics of a system diagrammatically to assist in the development of effective systems.

3. Flowchart symbols. A number of standard symbols are used in the construction of flowcharts (*see* Fig. 13.1). The symbols for the preparation of flowcharts represent various types of hardware device and/or processing activity, including input devices/type of input, action box specifying the nature of the computer activity, storage devices using disc and/or magnetic tape, and symbols which indicate the nature of the files used in each run. The symbols for program flowcharts distinguish between an action, i.e. a processing step using an action box, and a check or test using a decision symbol as a basis for conditional branching.

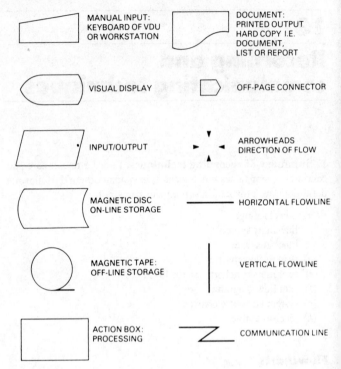

Figure 13.1 *Flowchart symbols*

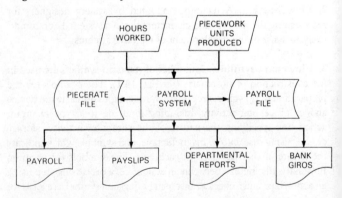

Figure 13.2 *Block diagram of a payroll system*

4. Block diagram. A block diagram, sometimes referred to as a 'system outline' or 'system function' diagram, is a low level flowchart which portrays the whole of a system in simple terms. It indicates the inputs, files, processing and outputs independent of operation details. (*See* Fig. 13.2.)

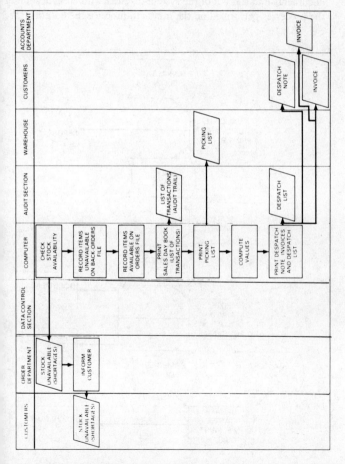

Figure 13.3 *Part of an order processing system: system flowchart*

5. System flowchart. This is a pictorial or diagrammatic representation of a system prepared on the basis of flowchart symbols. The term is used in its widest sense to describe any type of diagram showing the functions, data flows and the sequence of events or activities in a system.

The chart portrays a columnar analysis of the departments/functions concerned with a system and indicates the flow of documents into and out of the system together with an indication of the processes performed on the inputs to produce the outputs. (*See* Fig. 13.3.)

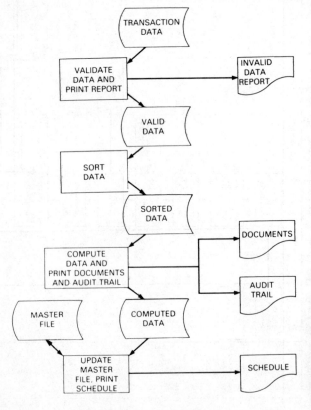

Figure 13.4   *Batch processing: computer runchart*

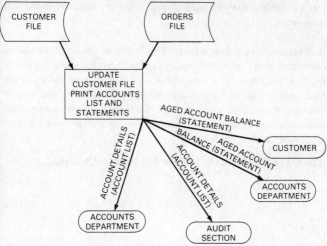

Figure 13.5 *Part of order processing system: data flow diagram*

6. Computer runchart. Computer runcharts are a specific type of flowchart for portraying the different elements of a system including system inputs, processing operations and outputs from each run. A runchart provides useful information to a computer operator as it conveys the nature of the hardware devices required for each run by means of appropriate symbols. Each run is shown separately with a brief narrative specifying the activities performed and its relationship with other runs.

Figure 13.4 is constructed vertically and progresses through the various tasks until the job is completed.

7. Data flow diagram. Data flows are portrayed on this type of diagram, pinpointing data origination points and destinations. Entities which send messages to or receive messages from the system are diagrammatically represented by a 'terminal' symbol; activities or processes which alter the data structure are represented by an 'action box'; data storage is represented by the 'on-line storage' symbol (*see* Fig. 13.5). Each symbol is allocated a name which is used for cross reference to the system documentation.

The construction of this type of diagram is concluded when each process box corresponds to a single task. Each of the major functions can be further analysed and shown in more detail on individual diagrams.

8. System structure chart. This type of chart is primarily concerned with logical relationships rather than procedural details. It may be prepared on a modular basis as shown in the example contained in Fig. 13.6 which outlines the procedure for assessing if stock has reached the re-order level. Such charts can be constructed on a hierarchical basis whereby elements at one level are controlled by an element at a higher level.

(For practical examples of flowcharting refer to Appendix 2.)

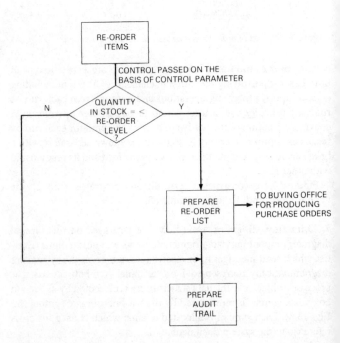

Figure 13.6 *Re-order routine of a system structure chart*

Decision tables

9. Decision tables. These may be used for analysing the conditions to be dealt with in a system and the actions to be taken when such conditions are present. A computer program for a specific application must incorporate conditional branching to other appropriate parts of the program to deal with the various conditions. A decision table is a means of ensuring that all conditions and actions are provided for without omissions.

There are two types of decision table – limited entry and extended entry.

Limited entry decision table
The structure of a limited entry decision table consists of four main sections.

(*a*) condition stub   } condition statement
(*b*) condition entries }
(*c*) action stub   } action statement
(*d*) action entries   }

The condition statement defines the conditions to be tested and the action statement the actions to be taken for specific conditions. The condition entries take the form of a number of rules consisting of both the condition entry and the action entry. Each condition and action stub contains a limited entry, that is an entry complete in itself. (*See* Fig. 13.7.)

When constructing a limited entry decision table symbols are used in the condition entry part of the table:

Y (yes) if the condition is satisfied;
N (no) if the condition is not satisfied;
— (hyphen) if the condition is not relevant to the rule;
X to indicate the action required.

A decision table may be prepared from a procedure narrative by underlining all conditions present with a solid line and all actions with a broken line.

Extended entry decision table.
An extended entry decision table only partially records conditions and actions in the stub. The remaining details are recorded in the entry sections. This type of table is more compact and less complex to

understand than a limited entry decision table but is less easy to check for completeness (*see* and compare Figs. 13.7 and 13.8).

		RULES		
	1	2	3	4
CONDITION STUB	CONDITION ENTRY			
SALES REGION CODE ≥ £50	Y	Y	N	N
INVOICE AMOUNT ≥ £1000	Y	N	Y	N
ACTION STUB	ACTION ENTRY			
DELIVERY CHARGES:				
ADD £15 TO INVOICE TOTAL			X	
ADD £20 TO INVOICE TOTAL	X			
ADD £30 TO INVOICE TOTAL				X
ADD £40 TO INVOICE TOTAL		X		

Figure 13.7 *Limited entry decision table*

		RULES		
	1	2	3	4
CONDITION STUB	CONDITION ENTRY			
SALES REGION CODE	≥ 50	≥ 50	< 50	< 50
INVOICE AMOUNT	> £1000	< £1000	> £1000	< £1000
ACTION STUB	ACTION ENTRY			
ADD AMOUNT TO INVOICE TOTAL	£20	£40	£15	£30

Figure 13.8 *Extended entry decision table*

Progress test 13

1. What is the purpose of flowcharting? (**2**)
2. What symbols are used for the construction of flowcharts? (**3**)
3. Specify the nature and purpose of:

(*a*) block diagrams,
(*b*) system flowcharts,
(*c*) computer runcharts,
(*d*) data flow diagrams,
(*e*) system structure charts,
(*f*) decision tables. (**4–9**)

14

Controls, standards, system specification and structured design

System controls

1. Underlying considerations. The extent to which security measures are applied depends upon a number of factors, amongst which are:

(a) confidentiality of the data;
(b) the extent to which it may be subjected to unauthorised access;
(c) the possibility of system failure;
(d) the possibility of corrupting files;
(e) the possibility of a file being stolen.

2. File security. Appropriate security measures should be taken to ensure that data is inaccessible to unauthorised personnel. It should also be ensured that adequate file security measures are implemented for 'dumping' (copying) data from a disc file to a magnetic tape file or another disc to safeguard against accidental erasure or corruption of the data, or theft of the file.

The security copy means that a file can be reconstructed by copying the data from the security disc or tape to the master disc. The security of tape files is accomplished by retaining the files of previous periods together with the transaction files so that they may be rerun to reconstitute corrupted or lost files. The files are retained on the basis of the 'generation' method, with several generations being kept.

3. Confidentiality of files: use of passwords. To prevent unauthorised access to confidential files a password is provided to bona fide users of the applications. The password, when input to the system, is compared with that stored in the software. Access is barred if the password is incorrect. When entered the password is not printed or displayed on the video screen for security reasons to prevent unauthorised personnel viewing the password and using it illegally.

Such applications usually have built-in enquiry programs to facilitate speedy information retrieval in response to queries. The data on the file is protected from alteration as amendments are not possible whilst the enquiry program is in use.

4. Security of databases. Alterations to a database are only possible by the database software, i.e. the database management system (DBMS), which prevents data being altered by applications software. Databases often incorporate a number of security measures, for example a user may be required to enter a user name before access is authorised. In addition, a password may be required to gain access to confidential information, and access to some parts of the database can be restricted to specified terminals. Each information owner must specify the names of users allowed to access his data and other information owners who can look at, but not amend, his part of the database. Individual pages can also be restricted by specifying user names.

5. Real-time security. Real-time systems are designed to deal with dynamic situations in order to control critical operations and are continually being updated as events occur. Such systems accept random input at random time intervals and the status of files changes accordingly making it necessary to implement security measures. These take the form of dumping all relevant restart and audit information periodically, say every two to three minutes, to tape or disc. The dumped data can then be used to restart the system in the event of a malfunction. Such operations are also provided with a second processor which is automatically switched into the real-time system in the event of the first machine ceasing to function for any reason.

6. Other controls and security measures. These include organisational, administrative, environmental, technological, sociological, procedural, operational and development controls, and are dealt with in more detail in Volume 1 of this book.

Standards and documentation

7. Purpose and objectives. The purpose and objectives of standards are for guiding staff in the general rules, conventions and codes of practice relating to the development, design, programming, implementation and operation of systems.

8. Standard methods relating to project control. The application of standard methods to the development of systems must stipulate whether the 'system life-cycle' or the 'structured' approach is to be implemented. The project control system will be structured to be compatible with the various stages of development, thereby providing a standard way of controlling all projects on the basis of a standardised schedule. This should enable the highest possible level of project productivity to be achieved.

9. System and program documentation. System and program documentation standards outline the way in which systems should be structured and the manner in which they should be documented. This applies to the method employed and the style adopted for the construction of procedure charts, system flowcharts, data flow diagrams, data structure charts, system structure charts, decision tables and runcharts.

Standards also apply to programming methodology with the use of standard coding sheets and the application of structured or modular techniques of program design. (*See* Appendices 2 and 3 for examples.)

10. Detailed design of system inputs, files and output. Documentation standards specify the way in which documents should be structured and compiled. Such documents contain details and specifications relating to the design of computer input (referring to the design of source documents and screen displays), output from the computer either as a screen display or a printed report, and the structure of master files. The primary purpose of such standards is to achieve a uniform, effective method of documentation to enable the systems to be designed in the most efficient way. (*See* Appendices 2 and 3 for examples.)

11. System continuity. The application of system and program documentation standards helps to achieve system continuity since it completely removes dependence on the details of the system existing only in the mind of a system designer. It is easy for the designer to forget points of detail, so it is imperative that all details of the current system and the proposed system should be committed to paper in various forms, i.e. document layouts and specifications as well as diagrammatically in the form of flowcharts, etc. This means that if design staff are ill or leave the company, then newcomers or existing staff taking their place can pick up the details of the project at the stage it has reached without much difficulty. This achieves continuity in the development of systems which is of extreme importance. Any disruption may cause delays to be encountered on the one hand, or on the other, inferior systems could be implemented which fail to attain their objectives.

12. Standards manual. The implementation of operations standards requires the compilation of a standards manual. Reference to the manual on points of procedure by operations personnel will ensure adherence to laid-down standards.

The standards should typically encompass details relating to the flow of work in respect of handling procedures for batches of source documents when received from the user departments, batch control and data conversion, security measures to be applied to the files after updating, work scheduling activities, archiving procedures, purging procedures in respect of retained files for security purposes, error control routines, output distribution routines, and so on.

13. Performance standards. High performance in a data processing environment is essential and performance standards are required and should be implemented for the control of output in order to ensure scheduled completion times are attained as far as possible. Input schedules should also be prepared for controlling input to the system to ensure it is received on time. This will prevent delays occurring and the build-up of work which would affect other jobs in the queue.

The cost of operations should be controlled to ensure operations are performed economically. This may be accomplished by the implementation of cost standards or the use of budgets. Run timings should enable the time spent on different jobs to be effectively controlled and provide the means of compiling job schedules.

14. Standards officer. The implementation and effective adherence to standards should be under the control of an overall standards officer. The duties and responsibilities of such a person include advising management and staff both in the data processing department and user departments as relevant to their activities in the data processing environment, in the use of the various standards. The results attained and methods practised should be monitored to ensure they accord with the relevant standards.

Staff suggestions for modifying established standards should be implemented if they provide the means of improving results and working practices. All modifications to existing standards and the application of new standards should be promulgated in a standards manual to ensure all details are fully up to date. The meaning and underlying philosophy of standards should also be discussed with appropriate personnel.

15. Communication and co-ordination. The major benefit of standardisation relating to systems methodology and documentation is the provision of a medium for discussion. Discussions of system details are improved between designers and users, designers and programmers and designers and management. Such discussions enable misconceptions to be removed and system features to be more fully understood. When personnel from the different functions affected by systems development are able to communicate then many of the inherent problems are more easily dealt with. It is always good practice to compile a 'glossary of system terminology' which further aids an understanding of the language of system designers and eliminates ambiguity in the understanding of terms being used during discussions.

NOTE: The National Computing Centre has developed a comprehensive set of standards embracing systems documentation, programming and operating.

System specification

16. Nature of a system specification. A system specification is similar to any product specification whether it is a hi-fi unit, television set, refrigerator or radio in as much as it specifies the features and characteristics of the system. A specification provides the interface between systems analysis and system design.

17. Summary of contents of a system specification. The specific details of a system specification depend upon the nature and complexity of the system, but a specification would typically include a number of sections as summarised below (and *see* also 11: **10**(*h*)):

(*a*) introduction;
(*b*) system objectives;
(*c*) system description;
(*d*) input specification;
(*e*) output specification;
(*f*) file specification;
(*g*) change-over;
(*h*) equipment;
(*i*) test data;
(*j*) program specification.

18. Sections of system specification.

(*a*) *Introduction.* This section includes details appertaining to the following:

(*i*)   name of the system;
(*ii*) glossary of terms used in the specification;
(*iii*) date of preparation;
(*iv*) statement of acceptance;
(*v*)   index to sections of the specification;
(*vi*) system relationships;
(*vii*) details of amendments to original terms of reference;
(*viii*) departments involved with the system;
(*ix*) standards of performance.

(*b*) *System objectives.* These include both the tangible and intangible expected benefits. *See* 18: **8–9**.

(*c*) *System description.* This section includes the following:

(*i*)   procedure charts and narratives relating to clerical systems;
(*ii*) data structure charts and data flow diagrams;
(*iii*) system flowcharts and computer runcharts;
(*iv*) decision tables;
(*v*)   system structure charts;

    (*vi*)   coding system;

    (*vii*) auditing procedures.

(*d*) *Input specification*. This section includes details of the following:

    (*i*)   name of system;

    (*ii*)   name of document;

    (*iii*) source and method of origination;

    (*iv*) details of data elements;

    (*v*)   frequency of preparation;

    (*vi*)   volume.

(*e*) *Output specification*. This section includes details of the following:

    (*i*)   name of system;

    (*ii*)   name of report;

    (*iii*) number of print lines;

    (*iv*) maximum size of fields.

(*f*) *File specification*. This section includes details of the following:

    (*i*)   name of system;

    (*ii*)   file name;

    (*iii*) file medium, e.g. tape: reel, cassette – disc: floppy, fixed or exchangeable;

    (*iv*) file labels;

    (*v*)   size of records;

    (*vi*)   record types;

    (*vii*) number of reels/discs;

    (*viii*) block size;

    (*ix*) field names;

    (*x*)   file security: privacy and confidentiality, use of passwords.

(*g*) *System testing and change-over*.

    (*i*)   test programs with test data;

    (*ii*)   testing procedures: dry runs (desk checking);

    (*iii*) pre-calculated results for comparison with results obtained from testing;

    (*iv*) procedure for system modifications;

    (*v*)   method of change-over: direct, parallel running or pilot;

    (*vi*)   change-over timing.

(*h*) *Equipment*. This section includes details of the following:

    (*i*)   type of computer;

    (*ii*)   peripherals;

    (*iii*) run timing;

    (*iv*)   computer utilisation;
    (*v*)   terminal utilisation;
    (*vi*) frequency of batch processing if relevant.
See 15: **3–15**.

Logical (structured) design concepts

19. Detailed description of system. This methodology creates a detailed description of a new system without considering hardware, software or other physical aspects. The logical system is designed on the basis of system objectives. This enables the system designer to determine *what* is wanted before deciding *how* it will, or can, be accomplished.

20. Logical (structured) approach. When applying the logical approach to system design it is necessary to construct a 'logical application model'. This specifies the messages which must flow to and from the users, or to and from the data stored in master files, and gives a description of the tasks which need to be performed to achieve the required data flows (*see* Fig. 13.5 and 11: **10**).

21. Stages of the logical (structured) design method. The stages of the structured methodology are as follows:

    (*a*) *Environmental analysis.* This is comparable with systems analysis as it is concerned with background matters relating to the area of the business for which an information system is to be developed. It embraces the collection, recording and evaluation of facts to enable the systems analyst/designer to gain an understanding of the business in systems terms.

    (*b*) *Functional analysis.* The business operations are analysed into logical groups of tasks called functions, together with the information requirements necessary to enable the tasks to be carried out. This stage specifies *what* has to be done.

    (*c*) *Logical design.*

      (*i*) *Application modelling.* This stage outlines the objectives of the system, analysing them into three categories: essential, necessary and desirable. It is also concerned with outputs, data and processes. (*See* **22–25** below.)

(*ii*) *Data modelling*. Data models relate to the data and information needs of a business. Data modelling is an important activity for integrating and/or segregating data elements into specific groups to form records. (*See* **26–27** below.)

(*d*) *Physical design*. This includes the preparation of an outline design of the system, producing what is referred to as a 'first sketch' of the system. This enables the design to be checked.

(*e*) *Prototyping*. This stage develops a conceptual model based on the first sketch of the physical system based upon the logical design. Its purpose is to demonstrate to the users the capability of the system to achieve their information needs.

(*f*) *Working system design*. This includes all the detailed design requirements relating to form design, dialogue design, input and output specifications, data storage, data control and design of coding systems. (*See* Volume 1 for further details.)

(*g*) *Provision of system specification*.

Application modelling

The process of application modelling involves a number of stages, as described below.

22. Stage 1: Definition of objectives. The logical objectives of the system and related sub-systems are defined. Primary objectives may be analysed into three categories, those that are essential, necessary and desirable. The essential objectives specify the primary purpose of the system which must be achieved if the system is to be effective. The necessary objectives support the essential objectives to enhance the effectiveness of the system and desirable objectives are those which would improve the system without affecting the achievements of the essential objectives.

For each category of objective it is necessary to prepare a data flow diagram as illustrated in Figs. 14.1 and 14.2. These illustrations show an integrated sales order processing system.

The three categories of objectives are specified as follows:

Essential objectives
Objective no.

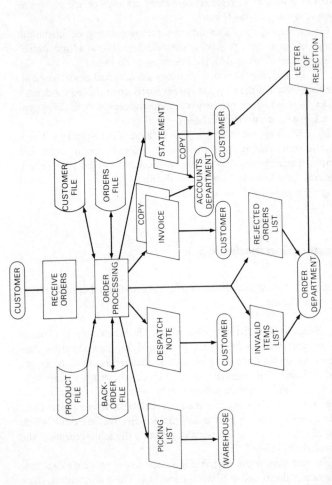

Figure 14.1 Essential objectives of an integrated sales order processing system illustrating data flows

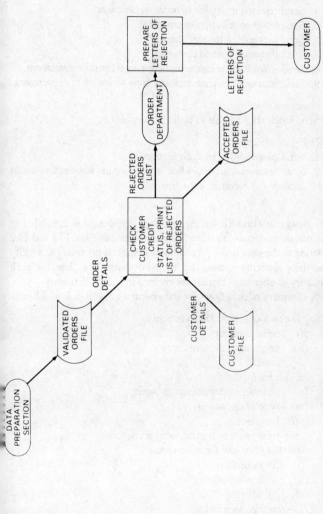

Figure 14.2 *Part of sales order processing system illustrating data flow diagram of essential objectives 4 and 5*

1. Receive details of orders and prepare batch control slip.
2. Send invalid items list to order department.
3. Store validated order details.
4. Send rejected order list to order department.
5. Send letter of rejection to customer.
6. Send picking list to warehouse.
7. Send despatch note to customer.
8. Send invoice to customer and copy to accounts department.
9. Send statement to customer and copy to accounts department.

Necessary objective
Send stock shortage list to order department.

Desirable objectives
1. Send despatch list to audit section.
2. Send accounts list including aged account balances to audit
   section and accounts department.

23. Stage 2: Data flows. At this stage the design is expanded to
include more detail of the data flows as outlined in Figs. 14.1 and 14.2
relating to the sales order processing system. It is necessary to specify
the data elements making up each outgoing data flow for each
category of objective. Details are entered in a data dictionary.

A summary of data flows for the essential objectives is as follows:

(*a*) *Batch control slip*. Data elements:
   (*i*)   serial number;
   (*ii*)   originating department;
   (*iii*) date;
   (*iv*)   system;
   (*v*)   number of documents in batch;
   (*vi*)   type of documents;
   (*vii*) hash total;
   (*viii*) total value of transactions (if relevant).
(*b*) *Invalid items list*. Data elements:
   (*i*)   order number;
   (*ii*) document number;
   (*iii*) type of error:
      —missing document,
      —missing field,
      —missing character in field.

Other outgoing data flows are dealt with in a similar manner.

24. Stage 3: Definition of data flows. This stage requires details of the origin of each data flow from the system for each category of objective. It necessitates identification of the data which can be input to the system, either obtained from storage or computed. Data derived from computation implies the need for a process to deal with this requirement. Details are entered in a data dictionary.

Data flows relating to the sales order processing system are outlined below.

(*a*) *Orders*. Orders are received by post in the order department from customers. They are then subjected to internal checking procedures to ensure details are correct and complete.

(*b*) *Batch control slip*. Prepared and attached to batches of orders by the order department. It provides data for controlling the processing of orders. Control data on the batch control slip is compared with control data generated during processing. This ensures that any mislaid documents are searched for and any corrupted data is detected.

Other data flows are similarly dealt with.

25. Stage 4: Internal processes including data maintenance. The system is now analysed into separate data flow diagrams for each segment of the system for each objective, indicating the data flows to and from storage and the functions of the various processes. This is followed by the preparation of a composite data flow diagram for each class of objective. It is also necessary to compile a structured list of functions.

Structured list of functions:

Objective	Function
1	1. Receive orders and prepare batch control slip.
2	2. Check details, reject invalid items (primary checks made by batch control clerks).
	3. Order department to make corrections.
3	4. Validate and store order details.
	5. Return invalid orders to order department for correction and resubmission.

Other data flows and functions are dealt with in a similar way.

Data modelling

Data models define the structure of files and make clearer the data needs of a business. They also help to segregate data into separate files or to integrate data structures when developing databases.

26. Normalisation. An initial requirement of data modelling is 'normalisation'. This is the process of separating items which are independent of each other into groups for recording in different files. It is necessary to ensure that each file has a 'key' which uniquely identifies the object which the data describes. Relationships between fields must be established, e.g. the relationship between the key field and the other fields of an object. All details should be recorded in a data dictionary.

In some instances a record relating to an entity may have two or more distinct groups of data which should be segregated into separate stores, i.e. files. As an example of this situation, details relating to an organisation's personnel may be classed as 'employee data' and may consist of the following elements:

(*a*) employee number;
(*b*) employee name;
(*c*) department number;
(*d*) monthly pay;
(*e*) tax code;
(*f*) gross pay to date;
(*g*) tax to date;
(*h*) standard deductions;
(*i*) bank sorting code;
(*j*) employee bank account number;
(*k*) bank name and address;
(*l*) marital status;
(*m*) age;
(*n*) sex;
(*o*) number of children;
(*p*) education;
(*q*) qualifications.

It can be seen that the employee data is more general than that required for payroll processing and can be grouped into two separate aspects, i.e. payroll data and personnel data (defined as the first normal form (1NF) – *see* Fig. 14.3).

(a) *Payroll data*:
  (i)   employee number;
  (ii)   employee name;
  (iii) department number;
  (iv)   monthly pay;
  (v)   tax code;
  (vi)   gross pay to date;
  (vii) tax to date;
  (viii) standard deductions;
  (ix)   bank sorting code;
  (x)   employee bank account number;
  (xi)   bank name and address.

The personnel data fields depend on the employee number key. The second group of data is:

(b) *Personnel data*:
  (i)   employee number;
  (ii)   employee name;
  (iii) department number;
  (iv)   marital status;
  (v)   age;
  (vi)   sex;
  (vii) number of children;
  (viii) education;
  (ix)   qualifications;

Changes to personnel data, such as that relating to marital status, number of children and qualifications, would not necessitate a change to processes which only used the payroll data. Neither would changes to payroll data, e.g. changes in monthly pay, tax code or standard deductions, necessitate a change in the processes concerned only with personnel data. The structures 'payroll data' and 'personnel data' do not contain repeating groups except for employee number, name and department which are necessary when accessing the personnel file particularly as departmental statistics are often required.

The payroll data contains dependencies which can be segregated into two data structures because bank data and employee data can be separated as illustrated below:

(a) *Employee primary data*:
  (i)   employee number;

    (*ii*)　employee name;
    (*iii*)　department number;
    (*iv*)　monthly pay;
    (*v*)　tax code;
    (*vi*)　gross pay to date;
    (*vii*)　tax to date;
    (*viii*)　standard deductions;
    (*ix*)　employee bank account number.
 (*b*)　*Bank data*:
    (*i*)　employee bank account number;
    (*ii*)　bank sorting code;
    (*iii*)　bank name and address.

An element of redundancy occurs since the employee account number is required in both structures for cross-referencing. This would be eliminated in a composite database structure, but for separate files benefits may be obtained because changes to bank details would not affect processes needing only to access employee primary data and vice versa. There also exist fields which can be derived from other fields because the bank name and address can be derived from the bank sorting code.

Normalisation of employee data has here generated three separate data structures. The process identified the fields which belonged to the separate groups with a minimum of redundancy, but some redundancy was necessary in the personnel data because of the need to use the key fields 'employee number', 'employee name' and 'department number' for cross-referencing and for sorting on the various keys within each file. This is defined as the third normal form (3NF).

27. Courting. This process is concerned with finding data which is held twice so that unnecessary redundancy can be eliminated. This could apply in a sales accounting system in which one data structure stores 'sales accounting data' in the sales ledger and another stores 'sales history data' in a history file. They would both contain common fields, i.e. customer code and product code. In addition, when items are despatched to customers it affects the 'value of sales' field in the customer record and the 'sales to date' field in the 'sales history' record. Both could be merged which would avoid inputting the same unit of data twice.

When common keys occur in data structures it is probable that the same data is being considered from two points of view which, in this instance, relates to despatches or sales history. This is indicative that the structures should be reviewed to see if there is a case for merging.

All details should be recorded in the data dictionary.

Progress test 14

1. Specify the underlying considerations for establishing the extent to which security measures should be applied to computerised systems. (**1-6**)

2. Outline the purpose and objectives of systems and program standards and documentation. (**7-15**)

3. List the main sections of a system specification, briefly indicating the content of each section. (**16-18**)

4. The modern approach to systems development is the logical or structured approach. Specify the stages of this methodology. (**19-25**)

5. What is meant by the terms: (*a*) application modelling, (*b*) data modelling. (**22-27**)

6. Define the terms: (*a*) first sketch, (*b*) prototyping, (*c*) working system design. (**21**)

7. Specify the four stages of application modelling. (**22-25**)

Part six
Systems selection and installation

15

Meeting the information systems needs of the organisation

Organisation appraisal

1. Organisation analysis. Meeting the information systems needs of an organisation is not an easy matter and initially requires a very careful analysis of the way in which a business operates. This in turn requires a knowledge of both the internal and external operating environments, and in particular of the structure of the functional organisation and the inter-functional relationships which exist. This means that a communications analysis study must be conducted to determine the information flows in the organisation and to highlight communications between functions in the internal environment. In addition, it will also specify the flows of information between the external environment – from customers and suppliers – and the internal environment, e.g. to the order office and buying office. It is also necessary to establish the nature of these information flows, the purpose they serve, the action taken from them and the contents of such information. Furthermore, it is necessary to assess the way in which such information can be collected, recorded, processed and communicated. This then is the theme of this chapter – the selection of a suitable computerised information system to meet the needs of the organisation in the attainment of its corporate objectives.

2. Wide range of options. The selection of the most suitable computer configuration is a difficult task because of the wide range of options from which the optimum system may be chosen. The optimum system is the one which will attain the required level of performance for both the current and foreseeable future needs of the business at a cost which is acceptable as regards initial purchase and the operating costs of which are economically justifiable on the basis of the return on the investment (*see* Chap. 18).

Appraisal of computer systems

3. Modularity. Computer systems are available which can be structured or expanded on a modular basis to suit the information processing commitment of various organisations. Computers differ widely in size, speed, output capability and cost, and it is necessary to select the most suitable combination of hardware – and indeed software – for the proposed applications. Computer systems should be selected with a defined migration path so that an initially small system can be built up by adding memory modules, faster peripherals, network facilities and further terminals as required to accommodate changes in the business environment, corporate strategy and mode of operation.

4. Large businesses, large computers. Large organisations require large computers with high speed processing power. On the other hand, medium-sized businesses require medium-sized computers, perhaps a minicomputer, whereas small businesses can function very effectively using a small business microcomputer.

Although this is only a generalised rule of thumb it is a useful empirical guide for initial considerations. The cost of a large computer can run into millions of pounds, mainly because of its vast speed of operation, communication and multi-programming facilities and the ability to support many terminals. (The cost is dependent, to some extent, on the number of terminals to be installed.) Minis, on the other hand, cost far less, but the actual cost is also a function of the range and number of peripherals required. Costs, as a general guide, are in the region of ten to thirty thousand pounds. A small but powerful business microcomputer costs in the region of two to four thousand pounds.

The amount of work involved in selecting a mainframe is much greater than selecting a micro. When choosing a mainframe a business will be concerned with the level of support provided by the manufacturer for the training of analysts, operators and programmers and the level of software support and availability of suitable database systems. The cost of installing, maintaining and operating a mainframe can also be quite appreciable. On the other hand, although a micro or minicomputer should only be selected after carefully appraising the various specifications in relation to the needs of the business, the situation regarding the cost of the computer and system development costs is not so critical. One of the major considerations with the selection of a micro is the availability of application packages rather than the degree of training offered.

5. Volume of transactions. The number of transactions to be processed is an important factor to consider in the choice of system as it allows an assessment to be made of the type of input device required and the nature of the processing techniques to be established. Relatively low volumes can be handled by a business microcomputer using keyboard data entry. This is a very slow method of data input, however, and larger volumes may necessitate the use of a small, medium or large mainframe using a key-to-disc method of data collection and validation. This then enables data to be transferred into the computer at high speed from magnetic disc.

6. Volume and length of records. Files containing many thousands of records of average length (in terms of characters (bytes)) will require a large computer system with high backing storage capacity and high speed data transfer capabilities. Applications consisting of 500–1000 records may be suitable for processing by microcomputer, though the capacity of floppy discs is limited compared to that of hard discs, i.e. Winchester discs. The larger business micros do have the option of adding Winchesters to the system for increasing the storage capacity and data transfer speed. If an application has a large file requirement, i.e. many thousands of records to be processed, several floppy discs would be required to record them, which would be very unwieldly as it would be necessary to change discs to deal with specific records stored on them.

7. Total processing time: use of benchmarks. It is necessary to assess the total processing time for each application to be processed. This can be calculated by multiplying the volume of transactions by the processing time for each process on each transaction. This may be established from benchmark timings which provide a basis for appraising the performance of different computers. The benchmarks provide timings for arithmetic computations, sorting routines, calling sub-routines and handling arrays, etc.

8. Processor characteristics. Processors function at different speeds, for example 2 MHz or 5 MHz. Depending upon the type of computer either 8, 16 or 32-bit processors are employed which indicates the size of number which can be processed at one time. In addition, the progression indicates that the more powerful processors have greater internal storage addressing capabilities. An 8-bit processor only has an address bus of sixteen channels which allows up to 64K bytes, i.e. 2^{16} which equals 65 536 bytes capacity. On the other hand a 16-bit processor often has twenty address channels which provides addressing facilities up to 2^{20}, i.e. 1 048 576 or one megabyte.

If integrated accounting packages and spreadsheets are to be implemented then a large internal memory capacity is essential in order to store the large number of instructions the programs contain. This may necessitate a minimum memory size of 256K or even 512K. The package specifications indicate the minimum memory size and other hardware requirements such as two disc drives. If applications require frequent processing of large volumes of data then a fast processor is essential. For applications with relatively little computational needs but high volume printout requirements – a common feature of business systems –then high speed printers are more relevant.

9. Operating system. The operating system used by a specific model of computer (e.g. MS-DOS – Microsoft Disc Operating System) is important because the more widely adopted (industry standard) operating systems have a vast amount of application packages already available whereas there is a scarcity of software for the less widely adopted operating systems. The reason for this is that software developers have an insufficiently wide market base for which to develop programs. The cost of specific software is also likely to be higher in such circumstances as the development costs are spread over a smaller number of potential users. It is also necessary to consider if operating systems have multi-task or multi-user facilities as this may be an important factor in the choice of system. (*See* Volume 1.)

10. Relative costs of hardware and software. In the early days of computers a major problem was the high cost of the hardware involved. The cost of hardware is now falling, mainly because of the great advances made in electronic technology which have reduced the size of computers whilst increasing their performance. As a result of this attention is being increasingly focused on the costs and time involved in developing software. It is important to appreciate, therefore, that while hardware costs are falling the labour intensive task of producing software is increasing and it is necessary for an organisation to minimise the problems and costs involved in software development.

The cost of developing software can be increased in some instances by employing programmers with insufficient experience for the projects under consideration. This situation can be remedied by employing skilled programmers conversant with structured programming techniques as these techniques allow program errors to be localised in one section of the program which is of help when program testing and during maintenance. Structured programming also achieves standardisation in programming methodology allowing continuity of development if programmers leave and will also increase programming productivity.

The use of pre-prepared computer programs (application packages) will also assist in reducing the time and cost of development. Some manufacturers provide *bundled* software, i.e. the costs of software are included in the quoted cost of the system. This means it is essential to assess the total cost of any proposed computer system covering both hardware and software. If software packages are to be paid for separately then their costs must be added to the costs of the hardware. Only then can true comparative costs be formulated. It is, of course, necessary to assess the suitability of packages for the proposed systems to be run on the computer.

Program generators can also be used for developing programs either by experienced programmers or by non-specialists in the operating departments. (*See* 19: **19–21**.)

Methods of selection

11. Assess strengths and weaknesses. It is necessary to assess the relative strengths and weaknesses of specific models and to draw up a short-list consisting of likely similar models from three or four manufacturers. The specifications of the selected models can then be compared with the facilities required and the objectives to be attained by the relevant business systems. For example, if a business has a large number of geographically dispersed offices, warehouses or factories then the number of communication channels a computer can control is of major importance. A *points rating* method of selection may be adopted whereby selected attributes are listed and points are awarded from a maximum of ten for each attribute with regard to its utility to the business.

A points league table may take the form outlined below:

1. Processor:
   (*a*) Number of communication channels
   (*b*) 8, 16 or 32-bit processor
   (*c*) Memory capacity
   (*d*) Number of peripheral ports for plug-in devices, e.g. serial or parallel centronic ports for printers, terminals and other devices
   (*e*) Speed of processor
2. Operating system installed:
   Industry standard or otherwise
3. Software:
   (*a*) Bundled or unbundled
   (*b*) Availability of suitable software for potential applications
4. Total purchase, lease or rental costs
5. Degree of manufacturer's support:
   (*a*) Installation support
   (*b*) Software support
   (*c*) Staff training services provided
6. Cost of maintenance agreement
7. Programming languages supported
8. Backing storage capacity
9. Multi-user/multi-tasking capability
10. Speed of printer
11. Other options, i.e. COM compatibility

For further aspects of this subject *see* Chapters 18 and 21.

Dealing with manufacturers and suppliers: tenders and contracts

12. Invitation to manufacturers. Obviously, when the system under consideration is likely to run into millions of pounds, the capital expenditure required for the investment in hardware and software cannot be taken lightly. In such situations it is normal procedure to invite a number of reputable manufacturers to tender for the contract.

13. Specification of requirements. The initial specification of requirements submitted to manufacturers would typically include:

(a) details of the systems to be computerised;

(b) volumes of data to be processed;

(c) communication requirements;

(d) number of terminals/work stations required;

(e) multi-programming considerations;

(f) standby needs;

(g) priorities;

(h) real-time or on-line (interactive) processing needs;

(i) content of reports required, their distribution and frequency of production;

(j) maintenance contract considerations.

14. System documentation. Flowcharts, organisation charts, document layouts and details of business operations would also be provided. Subsequent proposals are based on this information and the details are discussed by manufacturers' sales representatives with the systems staff and executives of the business. Such discussions also cover possible alternative solutions to the needs of the business. It is the prerogative of management to discuss these proposals with their systems staff who will subsequently recommend a specific course of action.

15. Proposals. The subsequent proposals will include a great deal of data relating to the nature and extent of hardware requirements, software support, the level of staff training to be provided and the extent of systems support and equipment maintenance. Detailed cost schedules relating to the various facets of hardware and software and the overall purchase cost will be included. It is important to consider the alternative financing methods available, including purchasing, leasing or renting, before arriving at a final decision. (*See* further Chapters 18 and 21.)

Progress test 15

1. An essential requirement in establishing the information system requirements of an organisation is an initial analysis of the business.

Specify the factors to consider in such an analysis. (**1**).

2. The selection of the most suitable computer configuration is a difficult task because of the wide range of options from which to choose. List a number of factors which may assist in the selection. (**2–10**)

3. State the use of benchmarks in determining the performance of different computers. (**7**).

4. What are the different characteristics of 8, 16 and 32-bit processors? (**8**)

5. Why is it important to establish the operating system used by a specific computer? (**9**)

6. When selecting a computer system it is essential to consider both hardware and software. Discuss this statement. (**10**)

7. How is it possible to assess logically relative strengths and weaknesses of specific computer models? (**11**)

8. What factors should be included in a 'points table' for the selection of a computer system? (**11**)

9. When selecting a computer it is normal practice to invite a number of reputable manufacturers to tender for the contract. What should be included in the initial specification of requirements presented to the manufacturers as a basis for tendering? (**12, 13**)

10. What other details would be provided to manufacturers in addition to a specification of requirements? (**14**)

11. Outline the details which would appear in subsequent proposals from manufacturers. (**15**)

16

Office automation and its effect on business

Changes of method and personnel policy

1. Velocity of change. Information technology is directly associated with the provision of facilities for improving managerial and corporate performance by the improvement of information flows within a business. Modern information technology is continually evolving but the fundamental issue is always the same – the application of the most efficient and effective means for achieving the objectives of the business. This has always been the concern of methods engineers in the manufacturing function and the systems analysts and organisation and methods officer in the administrative function. Additional problems to be contended with in the modern business environment include the extent to which competition is becoming fiercer and the increasing speed of technological change taking place amongst social and economic upheaval.

Changes in methods and practices have always meant the need to retrain and transfer personnel and to restructure the organisation to become compatible with the changing nature of business operations. It is these matters which are now considered.

2. Personnel policy. The personnel policy of a business provides the guidelines for the management of the human resources of a business. The nature of these resources needs to be reconsidered and policies restructured in view of the evolutionary nature of information technology. In such a situation it is important to maintain and improve human relations, and it is therefore mandatory for personnel management to discuss job changes and any redundancies with staff representatives. New job specifications will also need to be drafted and discussed including salary scales relating to any new job grades.

It is always good personnel policy to retrain suitable personnel for the new tasks to avoid redundancies whenever feasible. It may even be possible to transfer staff displaced by the new technology to sections of the business unaffected by these changes and which are likely to remain so for the foreseeable future.

When overstaffing occurs personnel policy may adopt various stategies to deal with the situation. Staff approaching retirement age may, for example, be offered early retirement to avoid making younger members of staff redundant. This would be a very effective policy in many instances as younger staff are more readily able to accept the challenge of new technology.

The evolutionary nature of information technology is changing the nature of office jobs. In some instances jobs have been 'de-skilled' as the detailed routines for performing the tasks are built in to the software (i.e. the programs) which perform them automatically. Many office tasks described in the past as 'pen pushing' activities are now 'push button' (or keying) activities. Details once recorded manually in ledgers are now data for updating (recording) on magnetic media (usually magnetic disc). Consequently skill is now required in keying in the data for processing rather than in the performance of the processing task itself as hitherto.

Recruitment of personnel needs to take these factors into account; good handwriting, for example, although still important in many instances, is not so critical when keyboard operations predominate. Well defined internal or external training can give individuals the necessary skills for new tasks employing hi-tech machines and equipment.

3. Areas of optimum improvement. Information technology is likely to affect all types and classes of personnel in all types and sizes of business. It is therefore necessary to know which areas of business activity and which categories of staff could most benefit from its implementation. If the efficiency of professional administrative staff – administrators, managers, accountants and so on – could be increased by providing improved technological facilities then this would ensure an optimum return on the investment compared with that attainable from relatively less critical categories of personnel.

Technological facilities for administrators, managers, accountants and other professional posts take the form of 'end-user' systems referred to as 'decision support systems'. These are discussed in detail in Chapter 22. In the absence of such formal systems accountants are tending to use microcomputers for ad hoc requirements such as general computations relating to the anticipated cost of projected staff increases, break-even calculations, cash flow analysis and stock re-order levels.

Effect on business administration

4. Accounting activities. The role of the book-keeper has largely disappeared except in the smaller business. Accounting staff are now largely concerned with preparing data for input to a mainframe computer and analysing the printed results such as payrolls and payslips, stock reports, lists of debtors and creditors, cost summaries, budget reports and labour turnover statistics, etc.

5. Administrative services. There exists a great deal of scope for improvement in the area of office services, embracing secretarial, typing, reprographical, postal, telex, filing, telephone, facsimile and other communication services. Information technology provides significant improvements with facilities such as word processing (improving secretarial, typing and some reprographic services); communication facilities in the form of electronic mail and digital PABX systems; databases in relation to filing and data retrieval systems, etc. Such advances improve business efficiency, eliminating unnecessary delays in communication between different parts of the organisation and dealing with routine filing and correspondence.

6. Management activities. Management is largely concerned with the planning, controlling and decision-making in the business and require timely and accurate information on which specific action or plans may be based. Any improvement in information flows and response times will therefore improve managerial performance and optimise the achievements of the business. To accomplish these improvements managers are now often provided with their own microcomputer with which they can access files directly and run modelling programs and spreadsheets as part of decision support systems. In addition, the valuable time of executives can be saved by the use of teleconferencing facilities so that they do not need to travel to a specific destination to participate in a meeting.

The home-based electronic executive office

7. Working at home electronically. The modern tendency will be for the busy executive not to have to 'go to work'! Modern technology makes it a feasible proposition to allow an executive to work at home without impairing his/her performance, whether the executive is a chief buyer, sales manager, stock controller, cost controller, personnel manager or a financial or management accountant.

The electronic equipment required to construct the electronic office consists of a portable terminal or computer, an acoustic coupler for connecting the terminal or computer to a public telephone line necessitating a telephone handset and connection point, and a monitor or domestic television set. The electronic office facilities are connected to a remote corporate mainframe computer and database by the telephone link. Alternatively, a portable computer may be used with a built-in RS232 serial interface for use with a printer.

8. Computer access. Access to the mainframe is achieved by dialling its number in the same way as a normal telephone call, and when contact has been established the executive keys in a password to gain access to the computer files. The computer is programmed to recognise each executive's password and which files they have authority to access. This type of configuration may also be used by executives away from home, mobile maintenance engineers and salesmen for establishing contact with the head office by means of telephone/computer/terminal communications.

9. Work station. A more comprehensively equipped home-based electronic office may consist of a work station with an electronic device known as a mouse (*see* **10** below) and a jack plug for connecting the work station to the telephone line to link up with the remote mainframe computer (*see* Fig. 16.1). The home-based work station can be linked to a local area network consisting of other work stations, microcomputers, word processors as well as the mainframe. The network supports electronic mail, electronic diary and file access via the database. The database allows data to be retrieved in respect of the master and/or functional budgets, cash flow projections, projected profit statements and balance sheets, stock lists, contract cost schedules, outstanding orders, premiums due for renewal, holiday

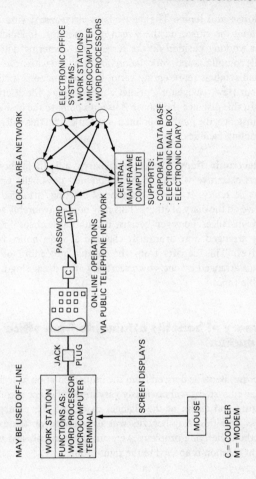

Figure 16.1 *Linking up with the outside world from the home-based electronic office using a work station and telephone*

packages due for payment, and any other facts according to the nature of the business and the responsibilities of the executive.

The work station can be used in an off-line capacity by the executive for *ad hoc* computations, word processing, message retrieval from electronic mailboxes, and program development if relevant. In addition, by using the appropriate software, the executive can resolve problems using a spreadsheet or other modelling program.

10. Mouse and icons. The mouse is an electronic device used for controlling the cursor on the screen of a monitor. It indicates the current working position on the screen when entering data. Some portable computers and work stations are provided with 'icons' which are small symbols representing various office functions such as 'in-tray', 'out-tray', 'calculator', 'printer', 'file copying', 'file deletion' and so on. In this instance the mouse is used to point to the desired icon. If, for instance, the mouse is pointed at the 'file' icon this will generate file handling facilities.

11. Electronic diary. An electronic diary is a useful facility for the business executive which can be maintained personally or by the relevant secretary. It records the time of meetings arranged by one executive on the diary of others. This may not be favourably accepted in many instances, however, because it could cause chaos if meetings already arranged were arbitrarily changed at short notice by other executives. This departs from the normal procedure of having meetings arranged by one's own secretary after discussing mutually agreeable times.

Summary of benefits attainable from office automation

12. Scope. Benefits derived from the implementation of technologically based systems will obviously vary in significance according to the nature and extent of the changes made and the nature of the business activities. Any benefits will also depend on the extent to which the underlying problems were analysed initially and whether the right solution is applied to the right problem.

13. Summary of typical benefits.

(*a*) Increased level of office productivity perhaps due to handling higher volumes of data with fewer personnel.

(*b*) Improved quality of decisions as a result of more purposeful and timely information flows.

(*c*) Integration of diverse activities either by multi-tasking or multi-access facilities using integrated software packages and computers of suitable capabilities.

(*d*) Problem-solving improved by decision support systems.

(*e*) Improved communications by the use of local or wide area networks.

(*f*) Information more easily accessible by means of databases and on-line information systems.

(*g*) On-line processing improves overall efficiency.

(*h*) Improved organisational control because of electronic mail and other electronic facilities.

Justification and management agreement

14. Evaluating benefits. One of the problems of obtaining management agreement to technological changes such as those outlined is the fact that most benefits are of an intangible nature. They are nevertheless of paramount importance to the business because they improve the effectiveness of the administration as a whole. The improvement of customer satisfaction is also of importance because without customers a business does not survive. Customer satisfaction is improved in a number of ways – *see* 18: **8–9**.

15. Global view. Management, quite rightly, like to see a reduction in operating costs resulting from a specific investment providing a rate of return in excess of normal levels. Unfortunately this is not always possible to calculate in figures, but an overall or 'global' view can be adopted. It logically follows that if more statements of account can be produced in a shorter time period by computer then cash flows should be forthcoming sooner thereby avoiding the need to incur costs on short-term overdrafts or loans. In addition, automatic stock control systems can reduce the level of stocks thereby avoiding excessive investment in surplus stocks and even alleviate the cost of stock obsolescence. It goes without saying that if more relevant and complete information is provided at the right time then management are able to make well informed and speedy decisions which would otherwise not be possible.

Progress test 16

1. Why is there continual change taking place in business as a result of information technology? (**1**)

2. Outline matters relating to personnel policy which would need reconsideration due to increasing use of office automation. (**2**)

3. What categories of staff are likely to be affected by information technology in its widest context? (**3**)

4. What is the likely effect of office automation on business administration? (**4, 5**)

5. How may management activities be improved by office automation? (**6**)

6. Outline the nature of the home-based electronic executive office. (**7–11**)

7. List the benefits you would anticipate from office automation. (**12, 13**)

8. What are the problems of obtaining management agreement to technological changes? (**14, 15**)

17
Systems installation, testing and maintenance

Planning the installation

1. Determine strategy. When preparing system installation plans it is necessary to take account of the complexity of change-over as this will have a bearing on the time required. Other matters to build into time schedules will be the time needed for training of staff, obtaining pre-printed stationery, system testing, time for resolving problems, file conversion and take-on of opening balances.

2. File conversion and take-on of opening balances. Many computer-based systems are of an accounting nature necessitating the conversion of files to magnetic media and the transfer of opening balances to the computer files. The time it takes to accomplish this task requires careful planning and control. The longer the transfer takes the more difficult it becomes to catch up with the current status of the system. This leads to frustration as personnel attempt to run both the current and the computer system on a disjointed basis. 'Catch-up' must be given priority while maintaining the current system in an up-to-date condition.

Very often records are converted from ledger cards on which transaction details are recorded by hand or posting machine to magnetic media by suitable encoding methods. Before conversion it is essential that the balances on such records as stock record cards, suppliers' and customers' accounts and employee payroll records are reconciled to ensure only correct balances are transferred to the new system. This creates a high volume activity and suitable arrangements must be made sufficiently in advance to avoid unnecessary 'take-on' delay. (*See* further Volume 1.)

3. System change-over. The methods of system change-over are outlined below to illustrate the various characteristics which need to be taken into account during the planning stage of installation. The methods relate to the way in which a new computer system will be installed or implemented.

There are three primary methods of change-over from the current system to a new computer system.

(a) direct;
(b) parallel running;
(c) pilot scheme.

Direct change-over

4. Nature of direct change-over. By this method the new system is installed without parallel running or pilot schemes. It is only suitable for relatively simple systems, but these are very rare as even the simplest of computer systems is in fact relatively complex to get up and running. Small business computers are more straightforward than mainframe installations but even so there are many complex factors to consider. All systems have inherent problems which do not always manifest themselves until the previous system has been dispensed with.

5. When to use direct change-over. Direct changeover should only be contemplated after considering all of the possible problems which can arise and their consequences. This is a high-risk method but may be adopted when the system is straightforward, when user staff are confident in running the system, and when time is short. This method may also be adopted when the current system and the new system are so dissimilar that parallel running is irrelevant. It may also be applied when the additional staff necessary for parallel operation are not available.

Parallel running

6. Nature of parallel running. This method requires the running of both the current and new system side by side on a fail-safe basis. The current system is not dispensed with until the integrity of the new system has 'been proved beyond reasonable doubt'. This is accomplished by comparing the results produced by the current system with those produced by the computer system. If they are in agreement the system integrity is assured.

As this is a fail-safe method it is costly because it is necessary to engage staff for running both systems side by side. This method also usually prolongs the testing period and delays system change-over, consequently time must be allowed for this factor. It is necessary, therefore, for a limit to be set on the number of cycles for which the two systems will run in parallel.

7. When to use parallel running. It may be said that parallel running should be adopted for all installations. Very rarely will the circumstances warrant the risky practice of direct change-over.

Pilot scheme

8. Nature of a pilot scheme. This method of system change-over also adopts a cautious approach. Resources are not committed to a company-wide implementation and the installation of a system is restricted to one location only. The results obtained from running this pilot scheme assist in determining the suitability of the system for other locations in the business. As an example, a pilot scheme may be implemented in one branch of a multi-branch business such as a bank or building society to assess its performance before it is introduced on a wider basis in all branches. This applies, for example, when putting branches on-line to a centrally located computer for dealing with daily branch transactions.

9. When to use a pilot scheme. A pilot scheme should be adopted when the system under consideration has far-reaching consequences on the efficient performance of key activities on a wide scale throughout the business. In such cases it is prudent to limit the implementation to one section of the business to be used as a proving ground. This will then avoid wide-scale disruption within the business environment.

NOTE: Whatever method of system implementation is allowed for in time schedules under the various circumstances which may prevail, it is necessary to consider two important factors:

(1) Do not prolong change-over to live operation unnecessarily as this will incur operating costs, perhaps because of extended parallel running.

(2) Do not change over to live operation too soon as operational inefficiency may be encountered due to insufficient familiarity with the new system as a result of inadequate training.

Test data and dry running (desk checking)

10. Test data and dry running. Prior to the installation of the computerised system test data must be prepared for live testing. It is also necessary to simulate the operation of the computer application before it is installed to detect any bugs. This is accomplished by desk checking or dry running which involves running through the program coding as the computer would do when processing actual data. This dry running may also be performed whilst checking related flow-charts and decision tables.

System monitoring and maintenance

11. Follow-up (monitoring). After the system has gone live and proved to be performing satisfactorily it is still necessary to monitor the system to ensure that no abnormalities occur and to remove the cause if any arise. It may be found that, although the system is achieving results as stipulated in the system specification, the system design does not provide for certain requirements. This situation will, of course, require system modification which will necessitate program recoding, recompiling and retesting. It will also require checks to ensure that system security and privacy are maintained at the stipulated level. Security checks must be made to ensure that there is no unauthorised access, for example, to confidential files such as the payroll and customer file and that access is barred to computerised automatic cheque writing facilities.

Periodic review meetings should be arranged to discuss future development of the system. Such development may take the form of system integration or links to a database.

12. System maintenance. Systems in their original form often outlive their usefulness because of the need to change business practices in accordance with changing economic circumstances and the introduction of new legislation. In addition, systems may be implemented initially on a stand-alone functional basis and management may later consider it a practical proposition to integrate related systems to avoid the input of data several times to each of several systems for different purposes. In addition, batch processing applications may be converted to on-line multi-user or multi-tasking systems. In other instances a database may need to be implemented to support the needs of a major business function or to rationalise the storage and retrieval of data for integrated systems.

Retraining personnel

13. Changing systems needs retraining of personnel. When manual systems are superseded by computerised applications there is a need to retrain existing personnel or recruit personnel from external sources for the new types of task which have been created. Before training can commence, however, it is necessary to select suitable personnel with the required aptitude and potential for specified tasks. Manual dexterity, for example, is essential for the expert manipulation of a terminal keyboard or keyboard data encoder, as this determines the speed with which data can be input for processing, the efficiency with which terminal operations are conducted, and the efficiency with which data can be encoded.

14. Training schedule. It is important to prepare a training schedule sufficiently far in advance of the date set for system change-over to ensure a smooth transition from one system to the other. It will also be necessary to arrange for personnel to be released from their current duties to attend the specified training courses or training sessions. Although this can disrupt the smooth functioning of the various departments concerned, it is a matter which must be accepted as a necessary requirement – the price to pay for future greater efficiency.

15. Mode of training. The mode of training provided will depend upon the nature of the activity. If, for example, the activity is concerned with the preparation of transaction data recorded on source documents into a form suitable for input to a computer this may require training on a key-to-disc or other data encoding system and will be undertaken partly by the manufacturer and partly by the systems analyst. The training of clerical support staff in the collection and recording of transaction details on new source documents is likely to be undertaken by supervisors after they have received instruction from the systems analyst. Alternatively, direct training may be provided to staff by the systems analyst. Similar considerations apply to the training of data control clerks who will be responsible for receiving, checking, recording and maintaining control of batches of work coming in from the operating departments.

The training of computer operators will probably require attendance at a manufacturer's training course which will provide direct operating experience of the type of configuration to be implemented. This will be supplemented by operating instructions provided by the programmer of the various applications. The chief programmer will receive guidance relating to the new systems from the program specification prepared by the systems analyst. This document specifies the requirements of the program to achieve the objectives of the system. When software packages are to be implemented programmers, computer operators and systems analysts may attend seminars sponsored by the software marketing company to obtain hands-on experience of such programs as integrated accounting packages, database management systems and spreadsheets.

16. Induction training. Apart from attendance at manufacturers' courses, on-site induction training may be arranged by systems staff to introduce the new technology to all relevant personnel. This would include departmental management as well as operating staff.

Induction training may be presented in a number of ways. Slide projectors may be used or photographs supplied to provide details of the hardware to be implemented, and the structure of the proposed systems may be illustrated by means of simple systems flowcharts. Lectures may be pre-recorded on cassettes to provide a general background, and video tapes may be used to supplement slides and cassettes. The initial step of an induction course may be a visit to a similar system in operation at a local company.

17. Monitoring the effectiveness of training. An essential factor of the follow-up routine after a system has been implemented is the assessment of the effectiveness of training. Further training may then be provided if this proves necessary or personnel may need to be replaced if they are unsuitable for the tasks assigned to them. The importance of an effective selection procedure has already been pointed out to avoid this situation (*see* **13** above).

Human factors in implementation

18. Participation of users. It is advisable to co-opt the services of personnel in the departments concerned with the project under investigation because of their experience in operating the current system and the detailed working knowledge they possess. They alone understand the idiosyncracies of the current system and are fully aware of its strengths and weaknesses. Stressing how important it is to incorporate their specialised knowledge into the system will help maintain user involvement at each stage in the life of a project.

The extent to which users participate in the design of systems will vary with the outlook of the management of the business, its management style – whether autocratic or democratic, for instance – and the viewpoint of trade unions regarding the interests of their membership. It is essential to build into the new system the 'strengths' of the current system while eliminating its weaknesses. In this way a more powerful and reliable system will emerge to suit current operational needs and practices.

19. Co-operation. Users and systems analysts should bear in mind that they both work for the same company and therefore have common aims and interests in the pursuit of operational efficiency. It is important that users appreciate that the purpose of the project is to improve the performance of the particular function as the current system is outmoded for current demands.

It is important to consider the feelings of the operating staff, and it is essential that they be reassured that it is not their performance which is in question. They should be informed that the system has been overtaken by new technology, and that it is important to implement the new system in order to maintain efficiency and competitiveness, and ultimately to enable the company either to remain, or become, economically viable, i.e. profitable.

It is important that user department personnel are aware of the nature of the proposed system with an explanation of how it differs from the current one. Subsequent proposals may recommend, for example, the implementation of an on-line order-entry system to streamline the order handling procedure so that the input of order details to the computer is speeded up to achieve a 24-hour turn-around time which is not possible with the present order processing system. This may be part of a plan to integrate the system with other related sub-systems to avoid entering data more than once and so speed up the preparation of invoices and optimise stock levels. Operating personnel must also be advised of the new jobs to be created, perhaps as part of a job enrichment scheme to make the work more interesting.

Progress test 17

1. What factors should be considered when determining the strategy for systems installation? (**1**)

2. File conversion and take-on of opening balances is an important activity in systems change-over. What factors are involved with this activity? (**2**)

3. Specify the main features of: (*a*) direct change-over, (*b*) parallel running, (*c*) pilot scheme. (**4–9**)

4. What is the purpose of test data and dry running? (**10**)

5. What is the nature and purpose of system monitoring? (**11**)

6. What is the nature and purpose of system maintenance? (**12**)

7. The implementation of new technology necessitates the retraining of personnel. What types of training are needed? (**13–16**)

8. Why is it necessary to implement a training follow-up routine? (**17**)

9. Why is it advisable to co-opt the services of personnel in the departments concerned with a project? (**18, 19**)

18
Costing of different systems options

Establish processing technique

1. Initial considerations. It is necessary to determine initially the type of processing required whether batch processing, on-line interactive processing on a multi-user basis, on-line data input combined with batch processing, distributed processing to provide for the widely dispersed nature of the business, or real-time control of critical operations. Having decided on the type of processing needed to achieve the information processing objectives it is necessary to determine the type of computer required and the necessary configuration to support the processing techniques – *see* Chap. 15. When alternative configurations are feasible then it becomes necessary to compare the various costs of the different options. The first step is the listing of all hardware devices, as shown below.

2. Batch processing v. on-line processing.

(*a*) *Hardware – batch processing*:

(*i*)　*Data preparation devices.* This may require a complete key-to-disc system consisting of several key stations, supervisor's console, miniprocessor and one or more magnetic tape and disc drives.

(*ii*)　*Input devices.* The choice is dependent upon the nature of the batch processing. An electricity or gas board, for instance, require optical mark and optical character reading devices, whereas a bank requires a magnetic ink character reader/sorter.

(*iii*)　*Output devices.* The choice of output device is normally the selection of a particular model of printer depending upon the printing speed required and other features such as carriage width.

(*iv*)　*Operator console*, which is normally a VDU and keyboard.

(v) *Backing storage.* A wide selection is available including fixed and exchangeable disc drives. Disc backing storage has a wide range of capacities and speed of data transfer. Magnetic tape storage requires tape drives which also vary greatly in speed of operation. Most installations require two or three disc drives and four or more tape drives but this is dependent upon the specific installation. Disc controllers are also required.

(vi) *Modems.* If remote job entry is necessary from dispersed offices then modems will be required for data transmission purposes. Leased private lines may be considered necessary instead of using public telephone lines which may cause problems when lines are engaged.

(vii) *Processor.* The selection of a processor will necessitate an evaluation of the internal memory capacity required. This is dependent upon the overhead required for the operating system, whether it is a multi-programming environment, and the extent to which integrated accounting packages are to be used which take up considerable memory.

(b) *Hardware – on-line processing*:

(i) *Input devices.* A number of terminals will be required depending upon the number of offices connected to the computer for multi-user applications. These devices replace the key-to-disc system used for batch processing.

(ii) *Communication devices.* If the on-line processing is a multi-user system then terminal controllers will be required. In addition, modems and multiplexors and front-end processors will be required, as well as private leased communication lines.

(iii) *Output devices.* Terminals are both input and output devices but in addition local printers may be required at each dispersed office for hard copy output needs and a printer(s) at the computer location.

(iv) *Operator console* will be required for monitoring the system.

(v) *Backing storage.* A widely dispersed on-line operation will require banks of fixed disc drives and disc controllers to support the file requirements of the various terminals.

(vi) *Processor.* A powerful processor will be required to support the multi-user environment as it must be capable of polling the lines to allocate time slots to each terminal. It requires a large memory capacity for storing the various user programs as well as the high overhead required for storing the operating system.

3. Software. It will be necessary to assess the extent to which application software is bundled or unbundled; if packages are to be purchased separately then it is likely that they will cost a lot more for the multi-user environment than for batch processing applications. *See* 15:**10**.

Capital and revenue expenditure

4. Capital expenditure. Expenditure incurred in the purchase of hardware and software may be classed as capital expenditure as they represent tangible assets which will appear on the balance sheet. Because the value of hardware is not used up in a single operation, it will be necessary to write it down each year as it is reduced through wear and tear (*see* **5** below).

Expenditure incurred on computer accommodation, including the cost of converting an existing building or constructing a new building, is also of a capital nature. Also included in this category is the cost of air conditioning equipment, storage racks for tapes and discs as well as desks and chairs. A larger computer will also require a standby generator in case of power failure and dust extraction equipment to avoid dust on the magnetic files which can corrupt the data they store.

5. Revenue expenditure – operating costs. This class of expenditure covers the operating costs incurred in running the computer system and includes:

(*a*) Leasing or rental charges of the computer or depreciation of machines and equipment if purchased.

(*b*) Licensing charges for the use of proprietary software.

(*c*) Establishment charges including rent of premises if not owned, rates, building insurance, heating, lighting and cleaning.

(*d*) Electrical power for running the computer system.

(*e*) Cost of leased lines.

(*f*) Rental charges for modems.

(*g*) Salaries of management and computer operations staff including data processing manager, operators, data control clerks, programmers, systems analysts and data encoders, etc.

(*h*) Payroll costs, i.e. national insurance of employer.

(*i*)   Holiday pay of staff.

(*j*)   Insurance premiums relating to computer system.

(*k*)   Operating supplies including magnetic tapes, exchangeable discs and printout stationery.

(*l*)   Training courses.

(*m*)   Telephone.

(*n*)   Travelling expenses.

(*o*)   General supplies.

(*p*)   Subscriptions and publications.

(*q*)   Maintenance costs.

(*r*)   Cost of standby facilities.

(*s*)   Bureau charges.

6. Once-and-for-all costs. It is essential to take into account what may be classed as 'once-and-for-all costs' which are incurred when developing a computerised system. Such costs include the cost of conducting feasibility studies, systems analysis and design, programming, and the costs incurred for running the two systems in parallel. Costs will also be incurred for changing over files from the current system to a form suitable for the computer when records are often converted from ledger cards to magnetic tape or disc files. Cost schedules relating to the various facets of hardware and software and the overall purchase cost will also be included.

It is important to consider the alternative financing methods available including purchasing, leasing or rental before arriving at a final decision. It will be necessary to ensure that the new system is performing satisfactorily and achieving the desired level of performance before discarding the current system. Such a 'fail-safe' routine incurs additional costs.

Intangible and tangible benefits

7. Investment in resources. Investment in computer systems or information technology in its widest sense must be recognised as being an investment in resources which must have an adequate return in the same way as any other investment. It is pointless incurring costs to produce information which serves no useful purpose and which therefore does not create benefits to the business.

Computer systems utilise resources in the same way as any other business activity because all activities in a business require manpower (personnel), machines, money and materials to accomplish tasks. The cost of the resources must be compared with what they accomplish. This is normally expressed in terms of benefits to the business.

Benefits are of two categories: tangible and intangible. Each of these categories is discussed below.

8. Intangible benefits. Many benefits are difficult to quantify. Cost savings or additional profitability cannot always be precisely defined. The following summary may help to put some sort of value on what may be described as intangible benefits.

Intangible benefits	*Questions to ask*
(a) More effective administration.	How much more effective?
(b) Improved customer satisfaction.	Due to what factor and to what extent?
(c) More optimum solutions to operational problems.	What does this mean in tearms of cost minimisation or profit maximisation?
(d) Improved forecasting techniques for strategic planning.	What will be the effect on sales?
(e) More timely information for the decision-making process.	What will be the effect of this in terms of cost savings and/or contributions to total profit?

9. Tangible benefits. Tangible benefits can be evaluated in the following way:

(a) The streamlining of information flows reduces the output of redundant information thereby improving administrative effectiveness generating a saving in staff costs of £X p.a.

Customers' accounts are paid more promptly due to the provision of more accurate and timely data relating to invoices and statements of account. This has improved the inwards cash flow by £Y p.a. which has the effect of reducing the interest on the bank overdraft by £X per month.

(b) As a result of implementing on-line enquiry systems customers are immediately informed of the information they require relating, for example, to product availability, availability of holiday accommodation and delivery dates, etc., and this enables them to respond accordingly without delay. This allows alternative choices to be selected, e.g. placing orders for alternative products or booking alternative holidays. This improves the profitability of the business by avoiding the prospective loss of profit as a result of not informing customers of available alternatives. This is assessed as an increase in profit in the region of £Y p.a.

(c) Due to the increased yield of material mix in the production of product X of Y% per week an additional profit of £X per week is achieved.

(d) Improved strategic planning as a consequence of improved forecasting techniques has generated additional sales of £Y p.a. and an additional profit of £X p.a.

(e) More timely information allows decisions to be taken in an acceptable time scale, i.e. response time, which has the effect of increasing operational efficiency in the use of resources thereby decreasing operating costs by £Y per week.

(f) More effective stock management reduces the level of investment in overall stocks by £X, in turn reducing interest charges on bank overdraft by £Y per month.

(g) More timely and accurate information relating to credit control improves cash flows and reduces debtors by £Y per month on average. This in turn has the effect of reducing interest on bank overdraft by £X per month.

10. Further considerations. Tangible benefits are more easily attainable at the operational level since control action taken to eliminate adverse situations or to take advantage of favourable conditions is very likely to have an acceptable pay-off. This is applicable in the following instances:

(a) reduction of excessive scrap to reduce production costs;

(b) reduction of excessive stock levels reducing the amount of money invested in stocks;

(c) improving the performance and efficiency of personnel by appropriate disciplinary measures;

(d) elimination of adverse expenditure variances by more effective control.

(*See* also **9** above.)

Progress test 18

1. How would you commence the costing of different system options? (**1-3**)

2. Explain the terms capital and revenue expenditure in the context of computer systems. (**4-6**)

3. Define the nature of 'once-and-for-all' costs in the context of systems development. (**6**)

4. Finance expended on computerised systems must be recognised as an investment in resources. Discuss. (**7**)

5. Distinguish between intangible and tangible benefits. (**8-10**)

Part seven
Software and hardware

19
Software

The nature of software

1. Definition. Software is the term used to describe program support which enables computer hardware to operate effectively.

A computer system consists of both hardware and software, and it is only by the intelligent combination of both that the best results are obtained. Hardware is a collection of machines which can only perform tasks when directed to do so by the software.

Software enables a general-purpose computer configuration to be transformed into a special-purpose system for carrying out a unique series of tasks for a number of different applications.

In general, software consists of the programs used by a computer prepared either by the manufacturer or user, but, specifically, the term embraces the operating systems and application programs supplied by the computer manufacturer.

2. Types of software. The nature of software is as wide and as varied as the nature of the work performed by computers. Software includes programs for accounting, financial planning and control, managerial planning and control, communications, word processing and utility programs. To some extent the nature of the computer determines the tasks to be performed, which in turn determines the type of software required. A small home computer will have a need for games programs or home utilities such as money management, budgeting or letter writing programs. Small business and mainframe computers will necessitate the need for software relating to accounting matters in respect of payroll processing, stock control and integrated accounting systems, etc. Most computers can utilise some form of word processing or database/records management software.

The types of software available for computers in general are summarised in Table 19.1.

NOTE: Matters relating to the principles of programming, levels of software, modular and structured programs and operating software are covered in Volume 1.

Table 19.1 Spectrum of Software

Nature of software	Type of software	Typical examples
System control	Operating system – general	Disc operating systems (DOS) UCSDp system CP/M UNIX DME/3 VME/K
	Operating system – networking	Designed to access local and networked resources (CP/Net)
Accounting packages	Application processing	Integrated accounting system General ledger Order processing Invoicing Payroll Stock control Sales ledger (sales accounting) Purchase ledger (purchase accounting) VAT records Business graphics
Managerial planning and control	Problem-solving and optimising packages	Bill of materials (BOMP) Production control (OMAC) Project planning and control (PERT)

Table continued

Table 19.1 *continued*

Nature of software	Type of software	Typical examples
		Deployment of scarce resources (optimiser)
		Linear programming (LP)
		Simulation
Financial planning and strategy	Financial modelling packages	General financial planning (The financial director)
		Financial strategy (Busicalc)
		Financial planning by use of spreadsheet (Visi-Calc, Micro Plan, SuperCalc)
		Integrated spreadsheet modelling, graphics, WP, database and communications (Silicon office)
Communications	Communications software	Access to Prestel and private viewdata systems (Owltel)
		Teletype communications (Micro-Linkline) (Interlink)
		Downloading
Various applications	Word processing packages	Text processing (WORDPRO, WORDSTAR)
	Various	Letter writing
		Diary planner
		Mailing list
		Card index
	Database/data management systems	Data and records management systems (many and varied)
System utility programs	Systems software aids	Editing
		Media conversion floppy

Table continued

Table 19.1 *continued*

Nature of software	Type of software	Typical examples
		disc to hard disc, tape to disc
		Dumping files
		Job control language (JCL)
		Program generators
		Sorting/merging
		Report generators
		Housekeeping
		Debugging/trace routines
		Disassemblers
		Assemblers and compilers
Sub-routines	Standard routines	PAYE routine for payroll processing
		Routines common to several programs
Home finance	Home management packages	Money management Budgeting
Games	Mainly for home computers	Many and varied
Miscellaneous	Programs for special purposes	Property management
		Civil engineering
		Builders
		Farm management
		Airline operations including seat reservation systems
		Hotel management and reservation systems
		Insurance
		Banking
		Building society administration
		Tour operators
		Electricity and gas boards, etc.

Applications software: integrated packages

3. General features of integrated packages. Integrated packages are sets of widely used programs, typically word processing, database, spreadsheet with graphics, and communications, this last for either micro-to-mainframe communications, a modem communications package or one for terminal emulation.

Each of the various types of program is dealt with separately later in the chapter. Paragraphs 4–7 below provide a brief introduction to the concepts and nature of integrated packages.

4. Advantages and disadvantages of integrated packages. When separate programs are in use, switching from one application to another entails the printing out of the results, changing the program disc, re-starting the computer and re-entering the data – a rather cumbersome and time-wasting exercise. Integrated packages enable the user to switch from one application to another without needing to change program discs. Data can thus be transferred from one file, e.g. a customer file showing amounts outstanding, and incorporated into text generated as a standard letter from word processing software. A fully integrated package therefore allows any user to access any part of it at any time. Multi-user systems also allow each user to access each part of the system as required.

There are disadvantages, however. Apart from the initial price of the software, there are also minimum configuration requirements. Typically these consist of:

(a) minimum system IBM PC 256K RAM;
(b) two 320K discs;
(c) colour graphics card;
(d) Winchester disc.

The Symphony package, for example, available from Lotus requires two double-sided floppy discs or a hard disc. The package is RAM-based and is very fast as a result. It requires a larger than normal memory, 320K minimum, because of this feature. The necessity for a large memory is to enable all the modules to be loaded into it so that they are immediately available in immediate access memory when required. The package does not use icons or a mouse but utilises the command line technique and menus. Switching between modules is easily accomplished and the user can generate customised applications through a command generator.

5. Typical packages available. Many packages are available to choose from providing an IBM PC or compatible computer is available. A selection of those currently available includes:

- (a) Lotus 1, 2, 3 and Symphony, both from Lotus;
- (b) Framework 11 from Ashton-Tate;
- (c) Knowledgeman from Data Base Experts;
- (d) Open Access 11 from Software Products International;
- (e) Works from Microsoft.

6. Single and multi-user packages. Some packages are designed to run on a single user basis but others are designed as multi-user or multi-user, multi-company systems using concurrent operating systems. The applications are usually menu driven and are user-friendly as they guide the user through each processing stage by means of prompts.

There now follows in paragraph 7 a summary of what may be defined as typical features of an integrated package. It must be remembered that some packages are designed for the small business and others for the larger business.

7. Important package characteristics. Prospective users of integrated packages need to be aware of the important characteristics to look for. These include those indicated below.

(a) *Commands.* A fully integrated package will incorporate a set of commands which will enable the user to run the various applications easily.

(b) *Windows.* This is a facility which allows the data of several applications to be displayed on the screen simultaneously.

(c) *Graphs.* This facility enables the transfer of data in a spreadsheet to that part of the program for producing graphs, e.g. bar charts, stacked bar charts, 'pie' charts, line graphs, scattergraphs and X–Y graphs.

(d) *Pipelining.* After windows have been displayed on the screen pipelining allows data of various applications to change several sets of data simultaneously.

(e) *Development software.* The provision of software by the manufacturers of integrated software to other software houses allows the latter to generate applications modules for interfacing with existing software to extend its range of capabilities.

(*f*) *Virtual memory*, whereby the system automatically uses all internal memory before buffering into disc memory.

(*g*) *Help facilities* of a context-sensitive nature.

(*h*) *Prompts* with context-sensitive explanations on choice of commands, parameters, etc., plus facility for switching off prompts when not required.

(*i*) *Task sequencing*, whereby commands can be stored in a file and used to control the sequence of applications.

8. Integrated environment. Some software enables users to configure their own combination of applications from individual packages which can then be run on an integrated basis. Data can then be interchanged under the control of the environment software.

Integrated accounting packages

9. The nature of IAP. An integrated accounting package is a suite of interrelated programs, often in modular form. Each module is designed to run on its own or as part of an integrated package. Accounting packages typically include modules covering the following applications:

(*a*) sales, purchase and nominal ledger;
(*b*) invoicing;
(*c*) stock control;
(*d*) payroll and costing;
(*e*) order processing.

The whole purpose of such packages is to streamline the accounting routines by allowing the transfer of common information or data relating to business transactions from one application module to another either directly or through a batch file. Additional benefits include the reduction in the number of staff concerned with accounting routines, increased accuracy of processing by computer, faster reporting and the facility for updating master files on a transaction basis as they occur.

10. Setting up. The first major consideration before attempting to run an integrated accounting package (or indeed any application package) is to study the manual provided with the discs containing the programs. The programs inform the computer of the processing stages required, but most systems are interactive, requiring the user and computer to intercommunicate by exchanging messages at various times.

The next important stage is to take copies of the master programs on other discs. This is a safeguard against the risk of damage to the discs as a result of a disc malfunction or a disc being corrupted by inadvertent overwriting. Program discs can be very expensive to replace.

Some suppliers of packages allow them to be used in a limited way for a trial period. Before it is possible to become operational it is necessary to contact the supplier to obtain a security code to prevent programs being used by unauthorised users. Prior to becoming operational copies of the converted master files should be taken as a security measure against loss or corruption.

The security code given by the supplier provides the key to the system and allows live operations to commence. When the code is typed in a menu is displayed for the selection of options according to the stage of processing reached or the routine to be processed.

The system must be tailored to suit the needs of the specific business running the programs. This requires the default parameters to be redefined as they are included initially on the basis of a standard set of business characteristics.

The contents of disc files need careful planning to obtain the best results from integration as they need to be structured to allow ease of data transfer between the various modules. If the modules incorporate sales, stock control and invoicing then a computer configuration with a double-sided dual disc drive could store all relevant data on the same disc to facilitate updating. When items are despatched to a customer an invoice is produced which contains information for updating the sales ledger relating to the value of the goods; the quantities despatched are updated on the stock file to facilitate stock control and re-ordering.

It is worth noting that it may be necessary to place files from related modules onto separate discs which are on-line at the same time but on different drives to avoid excessive head movement. For example, in an order processing system if the order file, stock file and customer file were on the same disc the heads would have to be repeatedly located to different cylinders to access the various records on the different files which would reduce processing speed.

When setting up the system it is necessary to establish whether pre-printed or blank stationery is to be used. A decision also needs to be made when to change the system over from that presently in operation. Usually it is best to commence the change-over at the beginning of a financial year as balances need to be brought forward in respect of debtors, creditors and fixed assets, etc. New accounts are also opened for sales and expenses at this time. If the system is changed over in the middle of a financial year any comparisons with previous years will require the addition of the figures from the previous system to those produced by the computer. This can be a very tedious process.

When a year-end date has been established it must of course be used consistently.

11. Coding. It is mandatory that all accounting systems should be structured on the firm foundation of an effective coding system. Coding structures are specified in a chart of accounts which indicates expense, customer, supplier, nominal ledger, and departmental (cost centre) codes which facilitate data transfers and postings between ledgers. Customers and suppliers are typically allocated a six-digit code, i.e. a code consisting of six alphanumeric characters, for example A12345.

Nominal ledger accounts may be structured on the basis of a three- or four-digit nominal code followed by a two-digit department code, e.g. A10001, of which the nominal ledger code is A100 and the departmental code is 01 (up to 99).

Some systems have pre-set account names and numbers for accounts which are considered common to many smaller businesses. Some packages allow for unsuitable codes to be deleted and additions incorporated using a nominal ledger maintenance program.

12. Data entry. Data entered is displayed on a pre-structured screen which facilitates data entry in a simplified and accurate manner.

Before entering data, however, it is necessary to select the relevant option from the menu which typically displays:

1. Starting a new week
2. Starting a new VAT quarter

3. Error correction routine
4. Cash receipts
5. Cash payments
6. Journal entries (for entries to the nominal ledger, sales ledger and purchase ledgers)
7. Reversal of journal entries
8. Standing charges
9. Month-end routine

The system may ask if the transaction is DEBIT or CREDIT and enquire if the entry is correct to which the user types Y or N. If N it is then necessary to make the appropriate correction, which may use the control key with a character key to clear the current entry or the new entry may overwrite the previous one.

Each time data is entered it is stored ready for printing out on a schedule for the provision of an audit trail.

A further message typically asks if there are any more transactions, to which the response is Y or N. If N the application reverts to the main menu for further data entry selections.

Some packages provide for account enquiries during data entry activities. The screen displays all the account details and a printout is provided if required.

13. Sales ledger module. A typical sales ledger module has a number of facilities including:

(a) open-item method for customer accounts;
(b) aged list of debtors;
(c) statements of account.

In addition a debtor control list shows accounts with an overdue balance or when a credit limit has been exceeded. A warning is displayed on the screen of any account which is overdue. Such accounts are automatically surcharged and letters printed of increasing severity. Cash receipts can be fully or partially allocated and predetermined parameters include cash discount rate and credit limits.

Selecting the month-end routine from the main menu clears all fully paid transactions leaving only the outstanding balances.

Integration with a word processing package is provided for in some packages to enable names and addresses from the sales ledger to be printed on standard letters for sending to customers with regard to overdue accounts.

The invoicing module normally provides for price selection, terms of trade and discounts. In addition, provision is made for variable rates of VAT – one of which being standard rate and the others exempt and zero rate.

14. Purchase ledger. The purchase ledger module typically provides for the following requirements:

(*a*) open-item accounting;

(*b*) aged list of account balances;

(*c*) random enquiry facilities;

(*d*) remittance advices;

(*e*) preparation of cheques and credit transfers;

(*f*) automatic listing of cheques due for payment based on pre-established credit period;

(*g*) mail shots;

(*h*) cash discounts (after agreement with supplier);

(*i*) inclusion of AUTOBAY, the National Westminster Bank's automatic payment system, and BACS, the Banker's Automated Clearing System.

15. Audit trail. For audit control purposes most packages print out details of transactions including the value and number of invoices, value and number of credits, cash transactions, amendments, deletions and additions, schedules of updated ledger accounts including the sales ledger and purchase ledger, etc.

16. File security. Typical packages also provide for the creation of back-up files for file security as part of the end of posting program. Prompts from the program inform the user when to load the discs for copying purposes.

17. Nominal ledger, profit and loss account and balance sheet. The nominal ledger is updated with the relevant transactions by nominal ledger code in respect of stock transactions, sales, purchases, pre-payments and accruals; plant and machinery acquisitions, disposals and depreciation; cash and payroll details, etc.

The trading, profit and loss account is processed showing typical details including sales, the cost of sales, wages, salaries, establishment charges, administrative expenses, depreciation, selling and distribution expenses, gross and net profit, etc.

The balance sheet is produced listing details of capital, reserves and current liabilities and fixed and current assets.

18. Reports. Most packages provide for a variety of reports, details of which can be stored on a predefined spooling file which allows print runs to be accomplished as one task at a suitable time after the period-end processing is completed.

Program generators

19. General features. The traditional method of preparing programs – by the initial preparation of detailed program flowcharts from which programs are written using a specific programming language – is being superseded to some extent by program development software which either uses a fourth generation language (4GL) and menus and prompts for guiding the user through all the stages of development, or structured programming techniques using interactive graphics. Fourth generation languages use a natural, near English, language several levels higher than a high level programming language, so it is more understandable by non-computer specialists who find it easier to use in the development of their own application programs.

The traditional systems life-cycle approach will be affected by this change of methodology. So too will the use of program flowcharting techniques, which are likely to be replaced by structured programming techniques which develop structure diagrams automatically (*see* **22** below).

20. System C. Program generators are software packages, an example of which is Sycero, marketed by System C Limited. The package may be used to develop traditional business applications such as payroll, accounts, invoicing and stock control. It can also be applied to the development of programs for applications where ready-made programs are unavailable. This type of package can also be usefully employed by experienced programmers since the Sycero programs are structured and documented in a manner which facilitates linking with other programs. By means of prompts and menus new records or files can be incorporated.

21. Building a program in seven steps. Using Sycero, as an example of a program builder or generator, the process of program building is seen to be very straightforward and can be accomplished in seven steps.

(a) *Plan the system.* Define the elements of the system to be created, the types of data to be input, the screen layouts for required displays and how many files are needed. Determine how the program is to handle the information.

(b) *Specify the system.* With the micro running proceed to select items from the main menu. By following the prompts proceed to define the types of files required and what items of information they will contain.

The menu offers the options shown in Fig. 19.1.

(c) *Draw the screens.* Having specified where and how data is to be stored it is necessary to specify how the data is to be entered and displayed on the screen of the computer. On each screen, type in

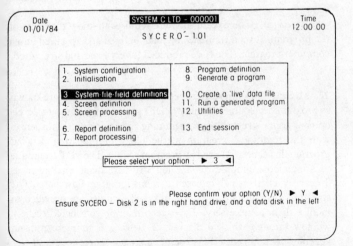

Figure 19.1 *Program generator screen*   *(Courtesy System C Ltd.)*

descriptions of the items to be entered and the exact position on the screen where the item is to be displayed. Graphics facilities can be used to sketch in lines and boxes giving the system a professional finish.

(d) *Check the data*. With the screens built it is prudent to incorporate a validation/verification procedure to detect when data has been entered incorrectly. Prompts indicate what needs to be input at any point, e.g. stock number, and also advise on the range of figures acceptable. Error messages can be displayed.

(e) *Define the program*. Define the program to operate on the data. There are certain standard operations which will almost always need to be carried out. Each system will require a file maintenance program to enter, amend and delete information. An enquiry program allows instant on-screen access to all data in any chosen form. Posting programs handle the logic of recording all transactions against a single item and updating files.

(f) *Produce the printout*. The system is now built and it is necessary to specify the printed output requirements, i.e. the report definition, or the formatting. The system provides facilities for defining where on a printed page columns are to appear, how they look, what their headers are like and so on. Column totals can be generated, each page can be numbered and printouts can be stamped with the date and time.

(g) *Generate*. The Sycero software requires to know the name of the program. It then translates the data defined and specified into a computer program. The code produced is very lucid and structured.

22. Michael Jackson structured programming. Software known as program development facility (PDF) provides for program development using structured programming methodology. It dispenses with the traditional program methodology of preparing detailed program flowcharts followed by program coding. The PDF technique uses interactive graphics to develop structure diagrams known as 'hierarchy' charts which replace traditional program flowcharts. The structure diagrams are stored on disc and facilities are provided to modify them as necessary. The screen may be considered to be a window through which a diagram is viewed. A simple command generates pseudo-code (JSP structure text) and source code ready for compilation or pre-processing. (*See* 11: **10**.)

Natural language database query system

23. Front-end to mainframe computer database. (The details which follow are based on material kindly supplied by Intellect Software International Ltd.) A natural English language database query and retrieval system, known as Intellect, is marketed by Intellect Software International Ltd and is used for query and *ad hoc* reporting by the first time end user, top executives and information centres. It is used as a front-end to mainframe computer database.

In effect the Intellect software trains the mainframe to understand the needs of the users. It harnesses the power of the mainframe, providing easy and instant access to information which speeds up data retrieval and analysis, reduces training costs, eliminates one-off programming and reduces batch reporting costs.

When a user asks INTELLECT 'How did copiers perform last quarter in each market?', it knows that both target (planned) and actual sales figures are necessary to compute the request (*see* Fig. 19.2). It retrieves the data, calculates it, averages it by branch, and presents it all to the user in a format that is clear and concise. All selection, database navigation, computation and result formatting is automatic.

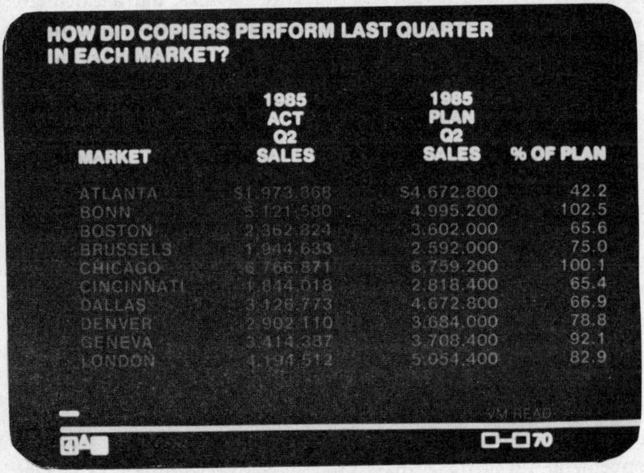

HOW DID COPIERS PERFORM LAST QUARTER IN EACH MARKET?

MARKET	1985 ACT Q2 SALES	1985 PLAN Q2 SALES	% OF PLAN
ATLANTA	$1,973,868	$4,672,800	42.2
BONN	5,121,580	4,995,200	102.5
BOSTON	2,362,824	3,602,000	65.6
BRUSSELS	1,944,633	2,592,000	75.0
CHICAGO	6,766,871	6,759,200	100.1
CINCINNATI	1,844,018	2,818,400	65.4
DALLAS	3,126,773	4,672,800	66.9
DENVER	2,902,110	3,684,000	78.8
GENEVA	3,414,387	3,708,400	92.1
LONDON	4,194,512	5,054,400	82.9

Figure 19.2   *Intellect screen   (Courtesy Intellect Software International Ltd.)*

Intellect runs as an application program under the following operating systems: IBM MVS/TSO, VM/CMS, MVS/CICS, DOS/CICS, MVS/Complete and DEC VAX versions under VMS.

24. DBMS and files. Those supported include:

(a) *Direct*: ADABAS, VSAM, Sequential files, SQL/DS; FOCUS, the leading 4GL DBMS, DFAM, Teradata DBC 10/12, DB2 and RDB.

(b) *Indirect*: IMS, DL/1, TOTAL, IDMS, ADABAS, VSDAM, ISAM, QSAM, Model 204, SQL/DS, DB2, DATACOMM DB and SYSTEM 2000.

25. Interactive lexicon. This enhances the natural language query capabilities because it enables users to customise Intellect to recognise their own words and terminologies. Lexicons are built with three key tools that are designed to automate construction of the initial lexicon and to make on-going lexicon enhancement fast and easy. The interactive lexicon is one of these and is the primary tool for developers.

26. Instant English. Instant English automatically converts the data dictionary information describing the database into a lexicon for Intellect's reference. This fully automatic process occurs instantly the first time Intellect accesses files to retrieve information. Instant English delivers immediate, fully functional, basic English access to any compatible database.

27. English definition. English definition allows users to create *ad hoc* definitions during an Intellect session. The system asks the user to define an unknown word in terms with which Intellect is already familiar and saves the definition for future reference. The user can enhance the lexicon whenever Intellect is used. The English definition feature is automatically applied whenever a user employs an undefined word.

28. Lexicon editor. The Lexicon editor allows the user to build and maintain lexicons for small and large database applications. A convenient 'fill-in-the-blanks' process enables the user to change immediately any definition displayed by the editor. The user can simply invoke this feature, or type in a request such as 'What is the meaning of "profit margin"?' and the user can change the definition to suit needs. Intellect can display a screen showing all the meanings of an ambiguous word, and the user can alter these meanings easily and quickly.

29. Key features of Intellect.

(a) Friendly interface.
(b) Rapid query development.
(c) Sorting.
(d) Summarisation, comparison.
(e) Statistics, percentages, ratios.
(f) Business graphics, high and low resolution.
(g) Security.
(h) Automatic report formatting.
(i) Screen painter report writer.
(j) Automatic lexicon building from DBMS schema.
(k) Interactive lexicon editor.
(l) End user definitions facility.
(m) Natural language database input/update in some versions.

Progress test 19

1. Define the term 'software'. (**1**)
2. The nature of software is as wide and varied as the nature of the work performed by computers. Discuss. (**2** and Table 19.1)
3. Outline the characteristics of integrated software packages. (**3–8**)
4. Outline the characteristics of integrated accounting packages. (**9–18**)
5. What is the nature and purpose of integrated accounting packages? (**9**)
6. What factors should be considered when setting up an integrated accounting package? (**10**)
7. State the nature and purpose of a program generator. (**19–21**)
8. Indicate the nature and purpose of a natural language database query system. (**23–29**)
9. What is the meaning of the terms: (a) interactive lexicon; (b) lexicon editor? (**25, 28**)

20

Applications software: spreadsheets, word processing and electronic mail

Spreadsheets

1. Spreadsheet definition. A spreadsheet is an electronic working sheet displayed on the video screen, i.e. the monitor, of a microcomputer or the screen of a work station. It is a problem-solving aid which is extremely useful for accountants, office managers, corporate planners and administrators, providing a speedy method of obtaining alternative solutions to a particular type of problem. Details are entered into the computer and recorded in predesignated rows and columns to form a grid of cells. The relationship of each cell in the grid can be defined for performing specific computations. Formulae can also be entered stating how variables (i.e. data) are related. It is also possible to perform 'what if?' computations to find out, for example, what would happen if sales were increased or decreased by a stated percentage, or if variable costs were reduced by a defined amount per unit, or the effect on the break-even point of increasing or decreasing fixed costs to different levels to accord with varying operating circumstances, etc. The spreadsheet may be used for cash flow computations, profit forecasts, preparation of profit and loss accounts, balance sheets and for break-even analysis, etc.

2. Operational features. To use a spreadsheet it is first necessary to load the relevant software, i.e. the spreadsheet program. The screen then displays a series of rows and columns. The top of the screen displays a row of letters which name the columns of the worksheet for columnar analysis or presentation of data such as a quarterly forecast profit and loss account or cash flow forecast. The initial display of column designations is A–H – *see* Fig. 20.1 – though the software,

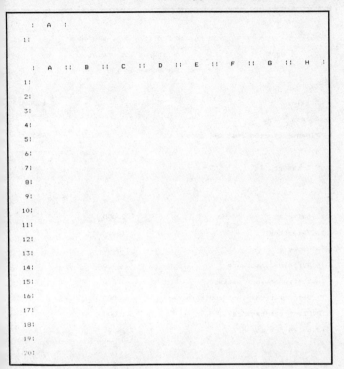

Figure 20.1 *Initial spreadsheet display of rows and columns*

SuperCalc, for example, provides for a total of 63 columns: A–Z and AA–BK. A column of numbers is shown down the left of the screen (*see* Fig. 20.1) which identifies the rows of the worksheet. The initial display is rows 1–20, but SuperCalc provides for a total of 254 rows.

A status line indicates the status of the active cell, and a prompt line specifies the width of the active cell, the amount of memory left and the cell reference. An entry line displays the information as it is entered by the keyboard.

It is important to plan the layout of the spreadsheet in advance to attain a professional-looking printout.

3. Entry of data. Data and formulae are entered into cells. Only *one* cell is *current* or *active* at any one time and is the one immediately

```
 :  A  ::  B  ::  C  ::  D  ::  E  ::  F  ::  G  :
1:              Trading and Profit and Loss Account
2:                       for the period ending
3:                       31st December 1987
4:                                                          £
5:Sales                                                 600000
6:less
7:Manufacturing cost of  goods                          450000
8:                                                      -------
9:Gross profit                                          150000
10:less
11:                               £
12:Salaries                      20000
13:Telephone                     10000
14:Rates                          5000
15:Building insurance             2000
16:Stationary and postage         2500
17:Depreciation:Plant and machinery  5000
18:Plant maintenance             11000
19:Sales promotion               20000
20:                             -------
21:Total expenses                                         75500
22:                                                      -------
23:Operating(trading)profit                               74500
24:less
25:Loan interest                                          10000
26:                                                      -------
27:Net profit                                             64500
28:                                                      -------
```

Figure 20.2 *Spreadsheet trading and profit and loss account*

available for use so that when data is entered it goes into the active cell. The row and column which contain the active cell are called the current row and column respectively. The active cell is designated on the screen by the cursor which is shown as a bar in reverse video. After data is entered the cursor is automatically moved to an adjacent cell which then becomes the new active cell.

Figure 20.2 shows a trading and profit and loss account constructed by locating the cursor at the desired printing positions, entering the relevant details on the 'entry line' and pressing the 'enter' key. The heading of the report is first entered and printed. The cursor is then located at A5 and the word 'Sales' is entered. It is then printed at the specified position when the 'enter' key is pressed. The cursor is then moved over to position G5 and the value of sales is entered. The gross profit is automatically computed by entering the simple formula G5 – G7, i.e. Gross profit = Sales *less* Manufacturing cost of goods.

All entries for the various expenses are made in the same way as the entry for sales – first the name of the expense followed by a relocation of the cursor and entry of the relevant value of the expense. The operating profit is computed automatically by entering the formula G9 – G21 in G23. The net profit is also computed in a similar way by entering the formula G23 – G25 in cell G27.

4. Further operational aspects of spreadsheets. A number of important operational commands are illustrated below, using Super-Calc as an example of a spreadsheet package.

(*a*) *Executing commands.* The slant key '/' is used for initiating commands. Each command is displayed by its initial letter, e.g.

B(lank) – Removes contents of cells.
D(elete) – Deletes entire row or column.
Z(ap)   – Clears worksheet and all settings.

When a command is entered in the form /Z the whole of the command is typed out automatically.

(*b*) *Erase or cancel command.* Press CONTROL key and Z, i.e. CTRL–Z. This erases the command from the entry line.

(*c*) *Clear the worksheet.* Type /Z. Type Y in response to the prompt.

(*d*) *Blank a cell.* Type /B. Type cell to blank, e.g. A1.

(*e*) *Enter text.* Precede with a double quote mark, i.e.".". Repeating text use a single quote mark, i.e.'.

(*f*) *Enter values.* (*See* **3** above.) Align cursor on required cell. Type the value and press the ENTER key. Align cursor on required cell for next value. Type the value and press the ENTER key.

(*g*) *Printing the worksheet.* If a copy of the screen display is required, i.e. a copy of the worksheet, the following commands are required:

(*i*) Type /O, i.e. the output command.
(*ii*) Type D to specify that printing is required as displayed.
(*iii*) Type 'All' to specify the entire worksheet.
(*iv*) Type ENTER.
(*v*) A PROMPT line displays the following: Enter device P(rinter), S(etup), C(onsole) or D(isk).
(*vi*) Select the required option, e.g. P for printing the worksheet on the printer.
(*vii*) Type C and the report will be displayed on the screen. If the worksheet is several pages in length it will be displayed one page at a time. Pressing ENTER will cause the next page to be displayed.

5. Bar charts. Values included in a spreadsheet can be converted into a bar chart. Values are first entered in a specific column, say column A (*see* Fig. 20.3). The procedure for obtaining the bar chart of the values shown in Fig. 20.3 is then as follows:

```
  :  A  ::  B  ::  C  ::  D  ::          E

 1:   2000
 2:   2500
 3:   3000
 4:   3500
 5:   1000
 6:   2500
 7:   4000

  :  A  ::  B  ::  C  ::  D  ::          E
 1:   2000                    ********************
 2:   2500                    *************************
 3:   3000                    ******************************
 4:   3500                    ***********************************
 5:   1000                    **********
 6:   2500                    *************************
 7:   4000                    ****************************************
```

Figure 20.3 *Bar chart generated by SuperCalc spreadsheet program*

(a) Type \ FG7 and press ENTER key:
   F = FORMAT
   G = GLOBAL
   7 = COLUMN WIDTH
Typing the initial letter F, G, etc. displays the complete word, e.g. FORMAT.
(b) Type \ FCE, 40 and press ENTER key:
   C = COLUMN
   E = COLUMN LETTER
   40 = COLUMN WIDTH
(c) Align cursor on cell E1. Type A1*40/MAX(A1:A7). This creates a value in column E which is proportional to the value in column A relative to the scaling factor (40 in this instance).

: A ::	B ::	C ::	D ::	E ::	F ::	G :
1:			BREAK-EVEN ANALYSIS			
2:						
3:						
4:Number of units				1000		1001
5:Selling price (£)				20		20
6:Variable cost per unit (£)				10		10
7:Contribution per unit(£)				10		10
8:				£		£
9:Sales income				20000		20020
10:Less						
11:Variable cost				10000		10010
12:				---------		---------
13:Contribution				10000		10010
14:Less						
15:Fixed cost				5000		5000
16:				---------		---------
17:Net profit				5000		5010
18:				---------		---------
19:Break-even sales (units)				500		500

Figure 20.4 *Printout of spreadsheet: break-even analysis*

(*d*) Next align cursor on cell E1. Type \ R,E1,E2:E7,A. This is the set of commands for replicating cell E1 in cells E2 to E7. To obtain E1 press ESC key which causes E1 to be recorded automatically, then enter the range of cells to be replicated. 'A' is the command for the system to 'Ask' if any adjustments are necessary.

The system then indicates that it is replicating and asks if A1 is to be adjusted to which the answer is Y because it contains a different value to the other cells. The system then asks if cell A7 is to be adjusted to which the answer is Y for the same reason. Scaled values are then displayed in column E.

(*e*) The scaled values are converted into bar chart format by the commands: \ FE E1:E7,*ENTER:

E = ENTRY

The bar chart is formed by asterisks varying in number according to the respective values in each of the cells in column A.

Further examples of spreadsheet printouts are given in Figs. 20.4, 20.5 and 20.6.

6. Developments. A recently announced spreadsheet, known as Access 4, has 216 columns by 3000 rows and uses virtual memory, i.e. it uses the disc drive as an extension to the internal memory. The size of the spreadsheet is limited only by the space available on the disc.

Software is now available which contains pre-formatted spreadsheets for 31 integrated budgeting schedules, from sales and profit projections and working capital requirements to full profit and loss accounts and balance sheets. The package also provides for 'what if' requirements. It works with Multiplan, SuperCalc 2 and 3, Lotus 123, Smart, VP-planner and 20/20. It runs on IBM, Apricot, Macintosh, Sirius, Amstrad 8256 and most other computers. The package is called Ultraplan and is marketed by Trinity Business Systems of Norwich.

Word processing

7. Characteristics of word processing. Word processing is primarily concerned with the normal typing requirements of a business as distinct from the reports produced by data processing systems. Whereas data processing is concerned with processing data

```
       Profit and Loss Statement for the year 1985

                        (£000s)

                        QUARTER

                   1       2       3       4     Total.

Sales           1000    1050    1103    1158    4310

Direct matl       50      53      55      58     218

Direct lbr       400     420     441     463    1724

Variable o/h     300     315     331     347    1293

                -----   -----   -----   -----   -----

Total var cost   750     788     827     868    3235

                -----   -----   -----   -----   -----

Contribution     250     263     276     289    1075

Fixed o/h        200     200     200     200     800

                -----   -----   -----   -----   -----

Net profit        50      63      76      89     275

(before tax)

                -----   -----   -----   -----   -----
```

Figure 20.5 *Printout of spreadsheet: profit and loss statement (after
removing row and column references)(Courtesy Apricot UK Ltd.)*

```
Profit per quarter                                    7.25
-----------------------------------------------------------

Quarter    Sales    Cost  S/Cost  O/Heads  T/Costs  Profit
-----------------------------------------------------------


J-M         5000      50    2500    1500     4000    1000

A-J         5363            2681    1500     4181    1181

J-S         5751            2876    1500     4376    1376

O-D         6168            3084    1500     4584    1584

-----------------------------------------------------------

Year/Tot   22282           11141    6000    17141    5141
-----------------------------------------------------------
```

Figure 20.6 *Printout of a quarterly profit forecast (after removing row and
column references)   (Courtesy Apricot UK Ltd.)*

in the most efficient manner, word processing is concerned with processing words in the most efficient manner.

The term word processing is currently used as a more fashionable or sophisticated name for automatic typing which was first used by IBM. Word processors may be called jet-age typewriters, but that is only part of the story as word processing equipment has electronic intelligence which generally consists of a processing unit supported by a separate memory. It is mainly this intelligence which distinguishes the word processor from the older automatic typewriter.

The technique is meant to provide increased cost effectiveness in respect of the typing requirements of a business. Technological developments are such that it is difficult for the prospective user of word processing equipment to keep pace with the changes taking place. It is this factor which makes the choice of suitable equipment very difficult, especially when this is linked to the need to learn how to use it in the most effective manner. There are many different makes and models on the market which have different characteristics and capabilities.

Word processing equipment should not be implemented without first conducting a feasibility study as it involves a change of method and necessitates the use of capital intensive equipment instead of typists. The method or technique of word processing is primarily for accomplishing the following office functions:

(a) transcription;
(b) editing;
(c) final typing;
(d) error correction;
(e) copying;
(f) storage and retrieval.

The equipment is designed to speed up such processes by making them more automatic.

8. Personalised letters. Word processors are of significant value where the typing requirements of a business consist of high volume routine correspondence such as personalised standard letters whereby standard paragraphs are stored on magnetic discs. The standard paragraphs and personalised details are indicated on a form by the author. The machine then prints the standard letter, reducing the detail entered by the operator to the personalised details only. It is this factor which achieves the main objectives of economy and efficiency because standard paragraphs are not constantly retyped at the speed of the typist but at the automatic speed of the machine, which can be in the region of 920 words a minute. With conventional typing the speed of a typist is greatly reduced by the need to make corrections and to completely retype text, as well as paper handling, interruptions and fatigue. A possible speed in the region of fifty to seventy words a minute is reduced to ten to fifteen words a minute by these factors. Extensive retyping also increases stationery costs, and produces additional wear on typewriter ribbons and the typewriter.

Lengthy reports or high quality text which usually require extensive editing and revision can be processed to advantage on word processing equipment as the correction of errors is simplified because to erase an error it is only necessary to backspace and retype the character, since characters are stored magnetically in the same way as in a computer system. This feature also enables words to be added to, or inserted on, any line on the magnetic media without having to repeat the remainder of the line. Word processing equipment offers no advantage in respect of short one-off letters or memos.

9. Benefits. The main benefits of word processing systems may be summarised as follows:

- (*a*) increased volume of output;
- (*b*) higher level of quality;
- (*c*) increased speed of output;
- (*d*) higher level of productivity;
- (*e*) reduced level of fatigue;
- (*f*) lower level of costs.

10. SuperWriter An outline of the essential features and operational details of the SuperWriter word processing program is given below in **11-17**. The details are illustrative only and no attempt has been made to cover all the finer attributes of the package. The SuperWriter program provides facilities to write documents, letters, forms and computer programs and store them for future reference, amendment and printing as stated above.

11. Operating instructions. The following details permit the use of the SuperWriter program:

1. Switch on the computer, monitor and the printer.
2. Load the applications disc.
3. Select SuperWriter icon or exit to DOS and type alongside prompt A>, SW, i.e. A>SW. Press ENTER key in either case.
4. MAIN MENU is displayed with the cursor located at the EDIT option.
5. Create a document by first pressing the ENTER key.
6. Prompt on screen displays: TYPE NAME OF DOCUMENT.
7. DIRECTORY – if the document name is not present the message is displayed DO YOU WANT TO CREATE A NEW DOCUMENT? (Y/N). Type Y for YES and press ENTER.
8. Type author name and press ENTER.
9. Screen goes blank with cursor in home position, i.e. top left corner.
10. Enter embedded headers and footers and embedded print formatting commands – *see* **13** and **14** below.
11. Type letter or other text.
12. Correct mistakes using control keys and codes.
13. Press ESC key; the screen then displays a series of options including:
    C D F G I M N R S X Z CR / TAB ESC ?
    Full details of these options are given in the manual.
14. Press S key to SAVE the letter or document on disc or Z to ZAP it (clear it) from the workspace.
15. Screen changes with the cursor located at SAVE DOCU-MENT on the sub-menu when S is typed.
16. Press ENTER key.
17. Document recorded on disc for future reference.
18. Screen changes to MAIN MENU for further editing, printing or document creation.
19. Press ENTER key.
20. Screen displays TYPE NAME OF DOCUMENT.
21. Type name of document to be edited or select option to PRINT as the case may be.
22. Screen displays READING (name of document).
23. Display of document on the screen.
24. Repeat routine from stage 7.

12. Main menu. The program functions on the basis of MENUS, the first of which is the MAIN MENU which lists six options:

1. EDIT document
2. QUIT SuperWriter
3. PRINT a document
4. CHECK spelling
5. DISK directory
6. Utilities

13.   Headers and footers. A header is standard text printed at the top of every page. A footer is standard text at the bottom of the page. They are usually applied when preparing lengthy documents or chapters of a book and carry such details as page number, date and document title, etc. They are embedded during the document or text entry stage at the top of the screen before any text is typed.

A command character (SLASH) is inserted in front of header details. A 'header' for these notes can be inserted before the text as follows:

SLASH header
SLASH right SLASH SuperWriter

14. Embedded print format commands. These are typed on the screen before text during the EDIT screen instead of using the print option in the PRINT MENU selected from the MAIN MENU. When the letter or document is printed the formatted commands are interpreted and executed but they are not printed as text. All print formatting commands must commence with a command character and end with pressing the ENTER key. Typical print format commands are:

LWn = Line width of n characters
TMn = Top margin of n lines
BMn = Bottom margin of n lines
LMn = Left margin of n characters (columns)
RMn = Right margin n characters from left margin
PLn = Page length of n lines

15. Inserting text. Text can be inserted from one document into another. This is a useful facility for reorganising documents, for example, or the chapters of a book. Either an entire document or individual screens can be inserted. The routine for accomplishing this is outlined below:

1. Move the cursor to the location where the text is to be inserted.
2. Press ESC key and then I.
3. Enter name of document from which text is to be extracted, i.e. inserted into another document.

When the document is found the first screen is displayed. The status line displays the prompts:

$$CR = Accept, A = All, Space = Skip, ESC = Quit$$

4. If the screen of text is to be inserted press ENTER.

16. Deleting text. SuperWriter has several control key commands to delete text. It also has a number of delete mode commands using ESC, D (*see* the manual for further details). When ESC, D is pressed the prompt line displays:

$$B \quad C \quad E \quad L \quad S \quad Command \; character \; Space \; ESC$$

Deleting a block of text requires several stages but is much faster than using a series of line deletions. To delete a block of text follow the routine outlined below:

1. Move cursor to the first character to be deleted.
2. Press ESC key and type command character to insert a marker.
3. Move the cursor to the character after the block of text to be deleted, i.e. the first character not to be deleted.
4. Press ESC key and type command character to add the second block marker.
5. Press ESC, D, B.

The status line prompts OK to DELETE *n* LINES? (Y/N) where *n* is the number of lines in the marked block.

6. Answer Y or N.

If Y is typed the text between the block markers will be deleted. If N is typed the block will remain in the text.

17. Copying a block of text to a separate file or document. The copy facility allows a block of text to be copied to a new document file on disc. This provides the means of separating a long document or chapter of a book into easily manageable sections or to extract blocks of text frequently used in other documents. The routine for accomplishing this is outlined below:

1. Move the cursor to the first character to be copied.
2. Press ESC key and type a slash to insert a block marker.
3. Move the cursor to the character after the block of text to be copied, i.e. the first character not to be copied.
4. Press ESC key and type a slash to add the second block marker.
5. Press ESC, C, W.
6. Type document name of new file.

The original file is unaffected. For further details the reader should consult the manual.

Electronic mail

18. General features of electronic mail systems. Electronic mail is a technique for distributing messages which have been created on a word processing or computer system. When a message is created on the sender's system it is electronically delivered to the receiver's system. The receiver reads the document from a video screen exactly as it was mailed.

Electronic mail facilities may be incorporated in local area networks or may be provided by a public service such as the Dialcom Electronic Mail service provided by Telecom Gold supported by British Telecom. In addition, digital PABX telephone exchanges, which form a catalyst for the electronic office as a whole, provide access to local area networks, mainframe computers, terminals, word processors, telexes, microcomputers, electronic printing equipment and electronic mail stations.

19. Advantages. Electronic mail has a number of advantages over normal postal services. The prime advantage is the speed of transmission far outpacing the time mail takes to be delivered in the post. There is in fact no delay in the receipt of a message except when the recipient is out of the office. With the normal postal service important mail may be lost or delayed, circumstances which can have drastic consequences to the business – perhaps losing important orders. It also has a number of advantages over the normal telephone system because a person does not have to be present at the time a message is transmitted by electronic mail, but does have to be present to receive a telephone call personally.

Electronic mail facilities resolve the following type of problem whereby, say, a production manager of a factory wishes to discuss a problem with the marketing manager but finds the telephone line is continuously engaged. This naturally causes a great deal of frustration apart from delaying an important decision. After repeated attempts to establish contact the telephone is answered by the marketing manager's secretary who informs the production manager that the marketing manager has left the building. In the meanwhile an important order on the shop floor is delayed whilst awaiting clarification of an important aspect of the product specification. With electronic mail facilities the original communication could have been transmitted and stored on the marketing manager's computer or terminal. The message would then be retrieved by the secretary and the urgency of the matter immediately noted and passed to the marketing manager for action.

20. Disadvantages. Messages can be transmitted to any location providing the terminal or microcomputer can be connected to the telephone system. Electronic mail is not suitable for all business communications or document handling needs, however. For example, it is not suitable for dealing with documents requiring an authorising signature, for long texts or for photographs.

21. Telecom Gold. This electronic system provides a number of facilities such as an electronic diary, word processing, a range of compilers for different languages as well as electronic mail. The system is used by thousands of people using either the telephone with 300 or 1200 bps modems or via the PSS (packet switch stream service). The system has six prime computers on the Dialcom network numbered from 79 to 84. Others include System 88 in Hong Kong, 15 in Germany and 11 in Singapore. It is a worldwide system.

It is necessary for a subscriber to 'log in' to the system by entering the relevant user-identification consisting of three letters (identifying the user group) followed by three digits (identifying the member of the group). A password is also required to be entered which is not displayed for security purposes. If the user-ID and password are accepted the user is allowed access to the system.

Each user of the system is allocated a 'mailbox' which is a segment of the computer's internal memory which stores messages. Each mailbox is labelled by the user's ID. The input of the command MAIL connects the user to the electronic mail system. The computer then expects the user to enter a command which can be either 'SEND', 'READ' or 'SCAN'. When SEND is entered the computer indicates that it requires the user to state the IDs of the recipients of the message to be sent. The READ command allows the user to read the whole of a message but SCAN only lists the sender of the message, the time, the date, and a single line describing the message content. If no messages are stored for a user then the response to a READ or SCAN command is the message 'No mail at present'.

Messages can be sent to a number of people without any physical reproduction of them. This would allow all nodes in a LAN (local area network) to receive the same message if it was relevant for them to do so.

A reply can also be attached to a message for automatic transmission back to the sender of the original message.

22. Prestel's electronic mail service. This service is known as Mailbox and can be accessed by 96 per cent of Britain's telephone users on a local call basis. Each Prestel client has a message Mailbox which is the electronic equivalent of a pigeonhole in which letters are placed in a normal postal service. The service maintains an alphabetical directory of clients which is updated every week. Bulletin board hosts and personal advertising sections quote a Mailbox number as the means of establishing contact.

The way in which Mailbox functions is as follows. Prestel is called up in the usual way, a message page is selected from the Mailbox index, and the recipient's Mailbox number and any message are entered. The page is then transmitted and the message is stored in the addressee's Mailbox. The addressee is informed of waiting messages the next time Prestel is contacted. Any number of messages can be stored in the Mailbox for any length of time.

The system provides a wide selection of page designs, including memo layouts and standard message layouts, etc.

23. Mailpost. Mailpost is a facility on the Telecom Gold mail system which provides a service consisting of a combination of old and new technologies. The text of a letter and the address of the recipient are transmitted by electronic mail to Mailpost's mailbox on Telecom Gold. The letter is then typed onto paper by the Mailpost staff who then post it in the normal way.

At the time the service was launched (around January 1986) a typical letter sent to a UK addressee cost in the region of £1 with Mailpost. Costs are also incurred with a once-only registration fee of £135. This includes the provision of a Telecom Gold mailbox.

The system is run by New Technology Systems which operates its own Telecom Gold user group. A complementary service is also provided to enable the non-Email addressee to reply to the communication. This is done by the recipient ringing up a Mailbox number on the ordinary telephone and dictating a message to Mailbox staff who then forward it electronically to the initial sender's Telecom Gold mailbox.

Progress test 20

1. What is a spreadsheet program? (**1–6**)

2. List several typical commands in a spreadsheet program. (**4**)

3. Illustrate a spreadsheet model by means of a diagram showing the screen layout of the selected application.

4. Describe the procedure for a spreadsheet model to convert values in a bar chart. (**5**)

5. What is word processing? (**7**)

6. Indicate some of the main operating features of word processing. (**11**)

7. Electronic mail is a technique for distributing mail electronically which has sometimes been created by a word processor. Outline the operational features of electronic mail. (**18–23**)

21
Computer hardware

This chapter should be read in conjunction with Chapters 15 and 18.

Categories of computer

1. Mainframe. A mainframe computer is the largest type of computer used for business and accounting applications. Large businesses usually require large computers to cope with the large volumes of data to be processed, usually of a routine nature, and the special reports required for business control and decision-making.

It is not possible to define with accuracy the general features of a type of computer as each model will have its own particular characteristics. However, for the purposes of illustration the features of the NCR 9300 are given here.

The NCR 9300 is completely modular, incorporating independent sub-systems and is suitable for use as a stand-alone computer system for the small business and for driving a large network of terminals. It is a 32-bit processor and its telecommunications, distributed data processing and systems network architecture (SNA) capabilities make it suitable for use in large DP networks. The electronics are based on a 32-bit VLSI (very large scale integration) chip which contains the circuits previously found in ten printed circuit boards on a single chip the size of a five pence piece. Its logic circuitry uses the semiconductor NMOS silicide process. The NCR 9300 functions under the control of the interactive transaction executive (ITX), an operating system with multi-programming facilities allowing the interfacing of multiple VDUs, industrial terminals, retail terminals and financial terminals both locally and remotely. The memory has one million bytes (one megabyte, i.e. MB) of RAM expandable up to four megabytes. The memory interface provides the logical connection between memory array chips and the address translation chip. It is capable of addressing up to 128 MB of main storage. An advantage of VLSI is that the computer is smaller in size, has a lower power consumption, greater reliability and costs less. It functions on the basis of internal and external virtual memory. It can support tape units with high transfer speed, various models of printer up to 2000 lpm, database management, report program generator, on-line program development, COBOL or BASIC programming language and is suitable for general business applications relating to accounting and information processing.

2. Minicomputer. This type of computer performs data processing activities in the same way as a mainframe but on a smaller scale. The cost of minis is lower and generally suits the needs of the medium size business. Data is usually input by means of a keyboard. As the name implies, a minicomputer is small compared with a mainframe and may be called a scaled-down mainframe as the processor and peripherals are physically smaller. Minis have a memory capacity in the region of 2M bytes whereas the larger mainframe has a capacity in excess of eight megabytes. In contrast, micros have a memory capacity in the region of 64–512K bytes. A typical mini consists of the following.

(a) Processor 512K–4M bytes.
(b) Video screen (display terminal – up to 24 in some instances).
(c) Integrated disc unit (often incorporated in processor cabinet). Capacity in the region of 80 to 320 megabytes.
(d) Cassette unit (often incorporated in processor cabinet).
(e) Printers with a speed in the region of 900 lpm.
(f) Tape drives.

Originally, minicomputers were developed for process control and system monitoring, etc. They were complicated to program and had minimal input/output capabilities as they were mainly concerned with 'number crunching' rather than handling large amounts of data relating to business transactions. However, they are now fully developed, powerful computers with a wide range of peripherals to perform a wide range of data processing and computing activities.

Minis operate faster than micros and tend to have sixteen-bit words whereas micros have tended to have eight-bit words. This is changing to some extent, however, as micros now have sixteen-bit words and thirty-two-bit machines are becoming available.

3. Microcomputers. A micro is a small computer consisting of a processor on a single silicon chip mounted on a circuit board together with memory chips, ROMs and RAM chips, etc. It has a keyboard for the entry of data and instructions and a screen for display purposes. It has interfaces for connecting peripherals such as plotters, cassette units, disc drives, light pens, a mouse, paddles and joysticks.

Micros are used within the smaller business for normal data processing applications such as stock control, invoicing and payroll for which packages are available. Micros are widely used in schools for educational purposes and on a personal basis for playing computer games for which there are hundreds of packages available.

The Apricot XEN is looked at in more detail in **4–13** below as an example of an up-to-date small business computer.

Apricot XEN

4. Configuration. The Apricot XEN is a powerful 80286 16-bit processor based microcomputer running at 7.5MHz, which, it is stated, can achieve processing speeds 60 per cent faster than the IBM PC/AT. The XEN has two basic configurations one of which has a twin 720K, 3.5″ microfloppy drive giving a total of 1.44 Mbytes of backing storage, with an internal memory capacity of 512K. The alternative configuration has a single 720K microfloppy drive with an integral 20-Mbyte Winchester disc and one Mbyte of internal memory. Both disc capacity and memory can be increased. Memory can be expanded by expansion cards for additional 4Mb of standard memory. Mass storage can be expanded by one internal 20Mb, 3.5″ Winchester, 10Mb external 3.5″ Winchester disc, or an IBM compatible external 5.25″ floppy drive unit. (*See* Fig. 21.1.)

5. Architecture. The architecture is based on gate-arrayed electronics and the latest 256K dynamic RAM chips. It has a single six-layer circuit board which uses the latest high component density technology to pack hundreds of individual components. An 80287 floating point co-processor is available as an option for applications which require fast processing of numeric data. A serial and Centronics parallel port are provided as standard.

Figure 21.1 *Apricot XEN computer* *(Courtesy of Apricot UK Ltd.)*

6. Communications. The Apricot XEN-COM system turns XEN into a powerful communications centre which provides access to databases throughout the world. Messages can also be sent by electronic mail and a telephone management system stores numbers in a directory for automatic sequential dialling. XEN can be used in an Apricot network environment and can communicate with all major mainframe and minicomputer systems.

7. Keyboard. The keyboard is 'soft' allowing all of the keys to be reconfigured at any time to suit specialist applications and to generate mathematical and foreign characters. It is functionally compatible with the IBM PC/AT.

8. Monitors. Various monitors are available offering different resolutions such as 800 × 400, 640 × 200 and 640 × 350 pixels.

9. Expansion. An expansion system is available which plugs into the XEN systems unit and enables two IBM PC or AT boards to be directly accessed by XEN.

10. Software support. It is supported by the world's largest software houses such as Lotus, Ashton Tate, Micropro, Software Products Inc., Digital Research, Software Publishing, Polygon and Microsoft.

11. Software applications. Software bundled with XEN includes MS-Paint, a drawing program, and MS-Write for word processing. Other software includes Card index, Notepad, Clock, Calculator and Appointment Calendar. A BASIC interpreter is provided for programming. Communications software is also provided.

12. Software compatibility. The importance of software compatibility with IBM is recognised and XEN provides an IBM-PC ROM BIOS Emulator which is a standard feature redirecting calls made by IBM software to the right devices within XEN.

13. User interface. The key feature of MS-Windows is MS-DOS Executive, the desk-top or user interface, which makes it easier to work with XEN (*see* Fig. 21.2). The MS-DOS Executive hides the complex operating system, replacing complicated commands and

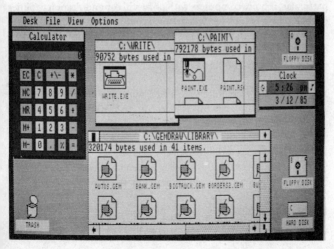

Figure 21.2 *Screen of Apricot XEN*   *(Courtesy of Apricot UK Ltd.)*

instructions with simple headings, drop-down menus, windows and icons. Within the combined power of XEN and MS-Windows multiple programs can be run allowing several tasks to be carried out on-screen simultaneously.

An optional trackerball mouse can be used which maximises the use of the latest generation of graphics based software interfaces such as MS-Windows. Complex commands can be executed by using the mouse to move data or select commands on the screen. Moving the cursor over the disc-drive icon, for instance, and clicking the mouse button will display within a window all the files on that disc. The cursor can then be moved over the entries and a file selected by another click of the mouse button.

Importance of type of business

14. Multi-national corporations. Large multi-national corporations with widespread operating units, banks, building societies and gas and electricity boards with widespread branches, and government offices require powerful processors capable of supporting many terminals on multi-access systems. Multi-national organisations, in particular, require computers with powerful communication facilities enabling them to transfer data between computers in different parts of the world at high speed. Distance is no object in the modern technological world in which business operates, especially with the extensive coverage of the globe by satellite communications.

15. Banks. Banks require specialised auto teller-oriented computer systems to collect data in respect of cash transactions through automated cash dispensing facilities.

16. Factories. Factory based operations require computer systems for capturing data relating to works orders and material movements by strategically located terminals throughout the factory.

17. Supermarkets. The needs of supermarkets with regard to point-of-sale equipment are covered in more detail in **28–29** below.

18. Real-time systems. Some types of information system are required for controlling critical operations in real-time, i.e. whilst the operation takes place. This applies, for example, to airline seat reservation systems which require powerful communication-oriented computers supporting a network of terminals for dealing with enquiries and seat reservations which immediately update the on-line information file. The required hardware also includes ticket and boarding pass printers and remote communication concentrators.

The primary objective of the system is to provide instant information on demand, and so prevent double, or over-booking of seats on aircraft. Such information systems must respond immediately to enquiries from dispersed booking offices and display the up-to-the-minute (second) status of seats on aircraft. In fact the status changes on the screen whilst it is being viewed thus providing the accurate information which prevents the booking of seats which have become unavailable.

This type of system is also used for planning fuel and other provisioning requirements for each flight as well as normal accounting routines.

Importance of processing technique

19. Type of processing technique. In addition to the type of business it is also necessary to determine the type of processing required, whether batch processing, on-line interactive processing on a multi-user basis, on-line data input combined with batch processing, distributed processing to provide for the widely dispersed nature of the business, or the need for real-time control of critical operations. (*See* 18: **2**.)

20. Processing objectives. Having decided on the type of processing needed to achieve the information processing objectives it is necessary to determine the type of computer configuration best suited to these requirements. Some of the hardware requirements for specific system needs have been outlined in Chapter 18 but for situations where alternatives are feasible then it is necessary to compare the various costs of the different options.

On-line processing

21. Purpose of on-line processing. The purpose of any on-line system is to provide an efficient means of processing business transactions using the techniques of information processing. This is accomplished by means of terminals connected to, and controlled by, the computer. The communication lines connecting terminals and computer enable the various departments of a business to be directly connected to the computer for specific purposes, depending on the nature of the terminal's function, whether for random enquiry facilities used for airline seat reservation systems, for on-line bank enquiry systems to check the status of customers' accounts, for enquiries from travel agents to the offices of tour operators for holiday details, or for on-line order processing.

22. Communication equipment: modems and multiplexor. Modems are necessary at either end of each communication line. If several terminals are connected to the computer they may be controlled by a cluster controller which connects each of them to a modem on a shared line basis.

The purpose of a modem is twofold as it acts as a *mo*dulator and *dem*odulator (hence the term modem). It is a device used for converting digital signals from terminals into analog signals for transmission by telephone line. When the signals are received from the terminal at the computer end of the line, another modem acts as a demodulator and converts the analog signals back to digital signals for input to the computer.

The lines may also be connected to a multiplexor, a communications processor or front-end processor (*see* **23** below). A multiplexor is a device which receives signals from terminals via communication lines which transmit at a relatively slow speed. The multiplexor accommodates a number of channels or lines within a single high speed line connected to the computer. This enables the computer to receive signals at a higher speed as the multiplexor batches together the signals from the various terminals.

Various types of software are required for the functioning of on-line systems. These include a powerful operating system to allow for time sharing, communications software supporting the operation of the front-end processor, and applications software.

23. Communications equipment: front-end processor. The function of a front-end processor in a system with a large number of remote terminals is to support the operations of a mainframe computer. It performs functions which the mainframe would otherwise have to do, such as code conversions, editing, validation, terminal recognition and controlling the communication lines. By delegating these functions to the front-end processor the mainframe is able to devote its processing capacity to high volume number crunching and other processing tasks instead of spending valuable processing time acting as a data transmission manager.

24. Location of terminals. It will also be necessary to establish whether the terminals will be within the same general location as the computer as this will determine the nature of the communication lines required for linking them together. If the distance is within, say, 4000 feet, then internal lines can be used, but if the terminals are geographically dispersed, perhaps in branch sales offices, then leased private telephone lines will be necessary in order to obtain exclusive use whenever they are needed. If the system is to depend on public telephone lines then delays could occur due to lines being engaged when required. This would tend to negate the purpose of such a system which is aimed at increasing administrative efficiency and avoiding bottlenecks in the processing of orders, eliminating shortages and reducing delivery delays.

25. Multi-access computer. If more than one terminal is envisaged for either an on-line order-entry system or other on-line applications then a multi-access computer would be needed which can effectively control the number of terminals on-line. The computer's memory capacity must be quite substantial to deal with multi-user operations as it needs to store sophisticated software by way of the operating system as well as the application programs.

26. Large capacity disc storage. It would also be necessary to have large capacity magnetic disc storage devices to take advantage of their direct access capability as an on-line order-entry system must be capable of direct access to records. For example, before an order is accepted it will be necessary to access the customer's record on the customer file for checking the credit status of the customer, and to access the product records on the product file to assess the availability of each item ordered, i.e. the stock status. The customer can then be informed of the delivery situation.

27. Other devices. A line printer would be required for printing documents such as picking lists, invoices, shortage lists, despatch documentation and various statistical reports. The speed of the printer required would depend on the volume of data to be printed out daily.

Point-of-sale equipment

28. Supermarket operations. The term 'point-of-sale' is used to describe the operating technique used for capturing transaction data as sales occur in supermarkets. Data is captured (recorded) using special laser scanners at check-out points. A scanner senses data printed in the form of a bar code on the label of the product which may be a loaf of bread, tin of beans, tin of tomatoes or other similar commodity.

The bar code used in Europe is the EAN code, i.e. European Article Numbering code. The light and dark lines of the code are converted into a number by the scanner which is sent to the in-store minicomputer. The computer looks up the number in its memory to identify the product and transmits the price of the item to the check-out terminal. The price is displayed and the price and description of the commodity are printed onto the customer's receipt, together with the total amount, the value of cash received (unless cheque or credit card) and the amount of change to be given. Other details are also printed including the date and check-out number, etc.

A system has also been developed which uses speech synthesising microchips to generate verbalised prices for customers. The digitised sounds are stored in a semiconductor store and released on the instructions from a bar code reader.

29. Equipment. The equipment required to operate a 'point-of-sale' system, depending upon its exact configuration, includes retail terminals at each check-out point (which can function as free-standing sales registers) equipped with a laser bar code scanner, a keyboard and VDU which can be used as a back-up system in the event of a malfunction with the bar code scanner, an in-store minicomputer

Table 21.1 Computer output methods

Method/mode	Media	Output device
1. Printed	Hard copy	(a) Character printers: (i) matrix (ii) daisy wheel (iii) thermal (iv) ink jet (b) Line printers: (i) barrel (ii) chain (c) Laser printers
2. Image recording: computer output on microfilm (COM)	Microfilm or microfiche	On-line COM recorder or Off-line COM formatted magnetic tapes
3. Visual	Screen display: text or graphics	Visual display unit (VDU) (work station terminal) or monitor of microcomputer
4. Graphical	Hard copy Charts, graphs or diagrams	Graph plotter or printer/plotter
5. Magnetic	For storing output for subsequent use, e.g. programs and files (a) Cassette tape (b) Large reels of tape (c) Floppy disc (d) Exchangeable disc storage (EDS) (e) Winchester disc (f) High capacity fixed discs (g) Data module	(i) Tape handler (ii) Tape spooler Tape deck Floppy drive Disc drive (exchangeable) Disc drive (sealed unit) Disc drive (fixed) Disc drive (sealed unit)

supporting the terminals at the various check-out points in the supermarket, a printer for printing customer receipts and, if the system is linked to an electronic funds transfer system, a data communication link to the various banks' computers for credit check enquiries and the transfer of funds.

NOTE: Matters relating to distributed processing, networks and multi-user systems are contained in Volume 1, as are matters relating to computer input, storage and output.

30. Computer output methods. Various methods or modes of computer output are summarised in Table 21.1.

Progress test 21

1. Differentiate between mainframe, mini and microcomputers. (**1–3**)

2. Outline the features of a modern mainframe. (**1**)

3. Outline the features of a modern small business computer. (**4–13**)

4. Summarise the main types of input to a computer (Chapter 5 and table 5.1)

5. When considering computer hardware it is necessary to consider the type of business and the various types of processing technique which may be applied. Discuss. (**14–29**)

6. Specify and indicate the function of the hardware devices required to support on-line processing. (**21–27**)

7. List the hardware devices required for point-of-sale (POS) operations. (**28, 29**)

8. Summarise the main types of output from a computer. (Table 21.1)

Part eight
Information centre and decision support systems

22
Computing for executives

Nature of an information centre

1. Information centre concepts. The concept of an 'information centre' is likely to be very widely applied as it enables personnel to gain access to their own data from a database by 'downloading' to their own microcomputer. The data can then be processed as required for a defined purpose without recourse to data processing staff.

2. End-user dedication. The 'information centre' is a department dedicated to 'end-user' computing and provides assistance and training to users to enable them to perform personal computing activities. In addition to downloading data from a database the information centre provides the tools, i.e. the software, which enable end-user processing to be accomplished. (*See* also **3–5** below.)

Decision support systems

3. Purpose of decision support systems. A decision support system, often referred to as an 'executive support system', provides facilities to enable executives to execute *ad hoc* computing to provide facts for problem-solving and making decisions. The facilities include a 'query language' for accessing the database, software for extracting data from the files of the mainframe computer for transfer to the user's computer, software for defining new records, a report writer and 'decision support' system, including spreadsheets, modelling programs, statistical analysis programs, data manipulation and graphics programs.

4. The complete executive. All this makes for a more 'complete executive' armed with the means for performing computations and evaluations which hitherto had to be carried out by mainframe computer utilising data processing staff or worked out very laboriously by slide rule or pocket calculator. This required a considerable amount of time, and often became very unwieldy if amendments gave rise to a snowball effect.

5. Evolutionary changes. In the past, accountants and other end users have used desk-top adding/listing machines, comptometers, slide rules, ready reckoners and pocket calculators, etc., for *ad hoc* requirements. Indeed some may still do so, but the modern accountant is dissatisfied with anything less than a Macintosh, Apricot or IBM PC.

This situation has come about since the development of the silicon chip which gave rise to a major revolution in the processing of business information, particularly for accountants. As a result of the chip, computers became smaller, faster, had larger memories with magnetic backing storage and were cheaper than anything before. The mystique which seems to surround mainframe computers does not appear to apply to microcomputers which the non-specialist soon came to understand and program.

Nowadays, few accountants or executives do not have access to a computer, either to improve the results they can achieve, or to save time in obtaining those results, or both. Computers are fast becoming 'Person Friday' to accountants and office staff generally in the quest for efficiency, particularly as computers can produce management information that much more quickly and accurately than any other method.

Decision support software

6. Deja Vu. Decision support software known as Deja Vu is marketed by Intelligent Environments Limited. The software enables information to be structured, analysed and modelled to assist in the decision-making process. It provides the framework for breaking down a problem into its constituent elements.

Decision modelling is a technique by which a series of options are evaluated against a set of criteria in order to determine the best option. Deja Vu allows the user to define the criteria and weight them in terms of their importance. The user's options are then analysed against the criteria. The software then ranks them in terms of best overall fit. In addition, sensitivity or 'what if?' analyses can be carried out by changing values and weightings. Results can be examined in summary form to compare and contrast the advantages and disadvantages of both sides.

Deja Vu makes it easy to store, organise, structure and reference information. Information is stored on pages and each page can be linked and cross referenced to any number of other pages. In practice the software works like a free-form database, allowing the user to reorganise and modify information without requiring the formality and technicality of conventional data management systems. Access paths make it easy to work with and around information by index, alphabetically, or by following logical paths around the model. Data entry is straightforward with full text editing and screen scrolling facilities. All the features of the package are easily accessed by means of pull-down menus and function keys.

7. System features.

(a) The system is available for IBM PC/XT/AT and 100 per cent compatibles.

(b) Runs in a minimum of 256K RAM.

(c) Three levels of help with 120 help screens.

(d) Pull-down menus.

(e) Context dependent prompts.

8. Technical details.

(a) All information is stored in a dictionary.

(b) Free text information search.

(c) Information can be points (criteria or notes) or options.

(d) Multi-level structures of points and options.

(e) Each point has own set of values.

(f) Weightings from +100 to −100, essential or forbidden.

(g) Handles missing or uncertain values.

(h) Options evaluated by points in turn.

(i) Statistical ranking of options.

(j) 'What-if?' analyses on weightings, values, criteria.

(k) Reporting and comparison capabilities.

Priority Decision System

9. Priority Decision System (PDS). A package known as PDS which stands for Priority Decision System is available from Work Sciences Associates. It is a computer-based support system for solving problems, making judgements and determining policies.

The package is menu driven. When starting up a three-part menu is displayed on the screen, offering either to solve a problem, make a policy or put a policy into practice. There is an alternative version with a Lotus-like screen format. PDS is available on IBM PC/XT/AT and compatibles, e.g. Apricot, Sirius, Victor.

10. Solve a problem. The packages can be used by an individual manager or a team and the program will combine the views of members of the team to produce a composite result. It helps decision-makers choose between alternatives systematically. To use the package it is first necessary to list the options (up to 20 choices). The personnel who can make the final decision must be named. Only a single name may be necessary but up to 20 can be included. The next stage is to assess how much influence each decision-maker is allowed in choosing between the various options. The final stage is to decide the option priorities which means choosing between alternatives.

The priorities and the decision-maker influences can be determined either by scaling, giving each person or option equal influence, use of intuition, magnitude estimation, or judgement analysis. PDS calculates the individual's valid priorities, pinpoints his/her inconsistencies, states whether he/she has achieved an adequate decision standard or not, produces the overall priorities of the team, and states the degree of agreement or conflict of the team. The whole problem-solving process takes 10–20 minutes from start to finish.

11. Make a policy. This is similar to the problem routine, but relates to objectives, criteria, or policy matters rather than options or operational problems. The 'policy-makers' must be named together with the influence they have on the policy – everyone is potentially a policy-maker in so far as they think about the issue at all. In choosing a computer, for instance, the criteria could include the type of processor chip (which itself is an expression of power in terms of speed of operation), operating system used, extent of the software available to run on the particular operating system, cost of mainte-

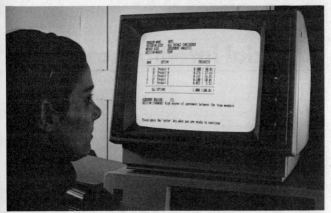

Figure 22.1 *Priority Decision System*

nance contract, reliability, upgrading option, cost of hardware and software, etc. PDS elicits the weightings of each criterion or objective for each 'policy-maker'. Again, this whole policy-making process takes 10–20 minutes from start to finish.

12. Policy in practice. When the two previous routines are stored on disc, access is available to the third facility of policy in practice. This permits the original option or options, such as the choice of a computer, to be systematically appraised on the basis of the policy criteria. A ranked and weighted list of options is then produced. This process can take 30–60 minutes on complex issues.

The PDS system provides a basis for consistent decision-making which will provide a greater pay-off than haphazard hunches. In addition it should remove inconsistencies in the appraisal of policy matters and resolve conflicts between managers as all points of view are taken into account on every aspect of every issue quickly. It should also save valuable time spent in operational and policy meetings. (*See* Fig. 22.1.)

Progress test 22

1. Define the concept of an 'information centre'. (**1, 2**)
2. State the nature and purpose of a decision support system. (**3–8**)
3. Outline the nature of decision support software. (**6–12**)

23
Artificial intelligence

Expert systems

1. Basic concepts. This type of system is also known as a 'knowledge based system' as it stores knowledge relating to a specific subject. Such systems may be used for diagnosing illnesses from symptoms indicated by the patient; diagnosing faults in complex machines such as computers, and for biological research into plant life, and so on. Expert systems belong to that branch of knowledge or information technology relating to 'artificial intelligence'.

2. Collecting knowledge based facts. The development of expert systems requires a high degree of co-ordination between researchers (sometimes referred to as 'knowledge engineers') and experts within a defined subject (also known as 'domain experts'). The experts from various fields of knowledge are interviewed by researchers to assess the best way of harnessing their knowledge into computer-based systems. This involves an analysis of how the experts themselves analyse a problem. The difficulty lies in attempting to establish some structure to the mass of details collected from the experts. A great deal of 'folk wisdom' emerges during the course of collecting knowledge and it is important that this is integrated into the expert system as it forms the grass roots of a specific topic.

Facts are usually best collected during an interview on a tape recorder for future in-depth analysis. Some interviewers attempt to remedy the lack of structure by carefully pre-formulating interviews, hoping to cover important issues without omission. Knowledge, however, does not necessarily come from the mind of the expert in such a structured form, and even the best thought out interviews do not always produce easily digestible sets of facts. Attempts to develop what is known as a 'knowledge engineer's assistant' are taking place with the primary aim of speeding up the development of expert systems. Work on this is under way by the Open University and British Telecom as an Alvey funded project. It is hoped that the assistant' software will assist knowledge engineers to impose some structure on the large amounts of details collected during the interviews.

The information collected is used to develop a computer program which follows similar thought processes and analytical techniques. The computer program has built-in rules for obtaining facts progressively until a suitable conclusion is derived using a menu selection technique.

5. Defining the nature of expert systems. It has been claimed that scientists have evolved expert systems which are more expert than the experts from whom they gained the knowledge initially. To the layman the nature of an expert system is something of a mystery as it is difficult to define and confusion has arisen in the combination of both scientific and computer jargon in publications relating to them.

Effectively an expert system differs from a normal computer program in that the latter simply consists of a set of sequential steps or instructions for achieving a defined result, e.g. a specific computation which is then displayed on the screen or printed out as part of a report or used to update a file, depending on the nature of the processing task. The instructions are repeatedly carried out until all the data has been dealt with. The instructions are rigidly adhered to, apart from branching requirements in accordance with conditions detected in the data – but even these are also rigidly applied.

Expert systems, on the other hand, are much more flexible in use and are controlled by in-built rules which are applied by the computer to suit specific circumstances. Additional rules can be easily added and others eliminated as the needs arise. Expert systems are more sophisticated than modelling or decision support systems and it is anticipated that decision support will be based more on expert systems in the not too distant future.

6. Menu/screen based information system. The example which follows was designed by the author as an aid for learning or revising the subject of data processing. The approach can, of course, be used

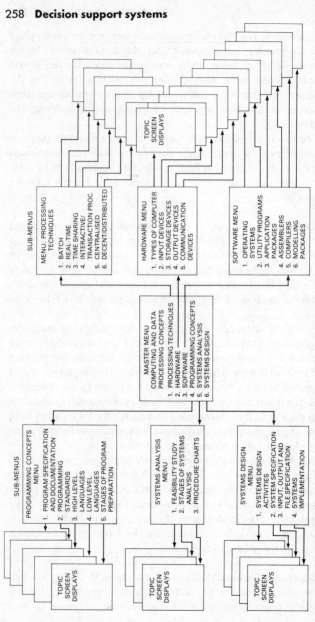

Figure 23.1 *Menu based information system showing hierarchical structure of menus*

for other subjects. It may be loosely called a knowledge-based system but a more appropriate title is 'A Simple Menu Based Information System' for deriving facts on the screen which have been incorporated in the program.

Figure 23.1 provides an outline diagram of the screens showing their structure. The master menu illustrates the main topics covered by the system which can be selected by keying in the topic number on the menu. This selection then generates a sub-menu which relates to the selected topic, for example the figure shows that the main topic PROCESSING TECHNIQUES is analysed into the following sub-topics on the sub-menu: batch, real-time, time sharing, interactive/transaction, centralised, decentralised/distributed. Further facts can be obtained by keying in the selection number as shown on the sub-menu screen.

This technique can be utilised by a student for a speedy revision course. The student could first select a topic from the main menu running through the points mentally before viewing the details on the screen. Alternatively, the details could be compared with revision notes made prior to accessing the screen displays. Any omissions or ambiguities can then be discussed.

Expert system builder

5. General features. Software is available for building expert systems, an example being the package called Crystal from Intelligent Environments Limited which runs on IBM PC/XT/AT and 100 per cent compatible machines. It is a personal computer-based system which can handle, structure and process up to 5000 rules in RAM. It is built for optimised performance and can deal with 500 rule inferences per second. Rules are typed in as notes or full sentences. The software requires no syntax, no rule language and no compilation. Rules can be found alphabetically, by paging or by partial string searches. The dictionary can be used to copy and select rules. Full text and graphic screens can be used to illustrate answers, advice or questions. Its authoring capabilities mean that the builder can use words and pictures to enhance the end-user system. Logical operators, AND, NOR and OR, etc, can be used in any combination at any level of the structure.

6. Menu based command language. Crystal has a menu based command language, providing for a detailed level of control in the logic, appearance and flow. The builder provides for an alphabetic dump of all the rules in the system together with each piece of evidence and text, with cross references. The evidence behind any conclusion is explained, as is the reasoning behind any question, and this allows the user to explore or navigate the entire logic of the system. The builder also employs an explicit rule structure. Conclusions are linked directly to evidence which in turn has directly linked evidence.

Progress test 23

1. What is an expert system? (**1–4**)
2. Define the following terms: (*a*) knowledge engineer, (*b*) domain experts, (*c*) folk wisdom. (**2**)
3. Specify the characteristics of software for expert system building. (**5, 6**)

Appendix 1
Examination technique

Examination questions in respect of information technology and information systems are often descriptive and aim to test the candidates' knowledge of how well-defined principles are applied to business situations or problems.

The subject is very wide and practical; candidates should always take care to demonstrate fully the wider implications of what may appear to be very narrow questions.

The examination candidate is recommended to observe the following points.

1. Read each question thoroughly before attempting an answer, in order to avoid any initial misunderstanding of the requirements of the question. A good answer to the wrong question does not score marks.

2. Allocate sufficient time to answering each question. It is fatal to omit an answer to a question through spending too much time on other questions. It is much better to have a fairly complete answer on all the questions rather than no answer at all on some of them.

3. Having determined the requirements of each question, the first one to be attempted should be selected. It is good practice before committing yourself to the answer paper to jot down main headings or topics to be covered on a scrap pad. By this means, initial thoughts may be clarified and the full scope of the question appreciated.

4. The answer may then be written on the answer paper, observing the following points.

(*a*) Write legibly to enable the examiner to interpret your answer easily.

(*b*) Show a good command of English, sentence structure and grammar.

(*c*) Outline the answer on the basis of topic or subject headings sub-analysed as appropriate as follows:

(*a*)
  (*i*)
  (*ii*)
(*b*)
(*c*)
  (*i*)
  (*ii*)
  (*iii*)

By this means the examiner can easily assess the points being made and can more readily appreciate their relevance and award marks accordingly.

(*d*) Keep to the subject and be as concise as possible without unnecessary padding – you either know the subject or you do not. Make sure you do before sitting the examination, even if only to save examination fees.

5. Allow sufficient time to read the answers before handing in the paper so that corrections can be affected.

6. Answer questions from your own experience whenever possible, as this shows the examiner that you are conversant with the subject in question.

7. Some answers require the presentation of a flowchart or other recording technique, and it is important to use drawing aids in their construction, i.e. charting symbol templates, coins (for circles), and a rule (for straight lines). Neatness of presentation is very important if maximum marks are to be gained. It is also essential to determine the type of flowchart required, e.g. procedure chart, system flowchart (runchart) or program flowchart.

Appendix 2
Construction of system flowcharts

1. Introduction. Question 1 of Section A of the CIMA paper Information Technology Management outlines the features of a business system and usually requires the construction of a system flowchart of the system outlined. The details of the system are presented in a logical sequence and it is advisable, in most instances, to construct system flowcharts accordingly. Practical examples of flowcharting are contained in Appendix 3.

2. Nature of system flowcharts. It is important to appreciate the nature of a system flowchart as distinct from a runchart. Details may be obtained by referring to Chapter 13. It is necessary to be aware that a systems flowchart portrays both non-computer and computerised operations whereas a run chart is restricted to computer activities only. (*See* Fig. 13.1 for flowchart symbols.)

3. Method of constructing system flowcharts. It is good practice to prepare initially a rough sketch of the system flowchart on a sheet of scrap paper whilst reading through the details of the system from the question. This approach enables the logic of the system to be established and simplifies the making of amendments, deletions and additions as the details of the system become progressively clearer. It is much easier to modify a rough sketch rather than the final flowchart presented to the examiner.

Subsequently, the system flowchart may be committed to the answer paper in a confident manner using a flowchart template. This drawing aid provides standard flowchart symbols. If you do not possess a template do not draw flowcharts free-hand as this presents an unprofessional appearance and will lose marks accordingly. Use a coin and rule if nothing else is available.

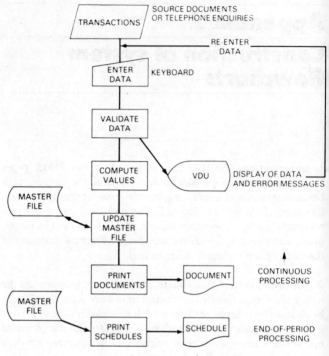

Figure A1 *System flowchart: interactive (on-line) processing*

A system flowchart normally commences with an 'input' of data. In some instances this may be details of a transaction communicated by telephone to a telesales person who is equipped with a terminal keyboard linked to a computer to deal with such enquiries and/or the input of sales order details. The keyboard is drawn using the relevant symbol on the template. This form of processing is referred to as on-line interactive processing and is depicted in Fig. A1.

For batch processing systems the initial data relating to business transactions may be in the form of batches of 'source' documents which may be portrayed by the input/output symbol. Data may then be encoded either to magnetic disc or magnetic tape. The keyboard symbol may be used for this purpose. If data is recorded on disc a 'key-to-disc' data preparation system may be used for converting the data to magnetic disc. This approach enables data to be input at high speed thereby saving time. It would take much longer to input the same volume of transactions by keyboard and cause the processor to be inactive for a considerable proportion of the total processing time. Figure A2 outlines the structure and activities relating to a batch processing system, including data preparation activities.

Processing steps are shown by the action box symbol which specifies the 'activity' or 'operation' to be performed by the computer at that specific stage of processing. After data is processed an 'output' is produced which is depicted by the relevant symbol, e.g. a magnetic disc or magnetic tape symbol if the output is to a file such as a work file or master file. Alternatively the output may be visually displayed

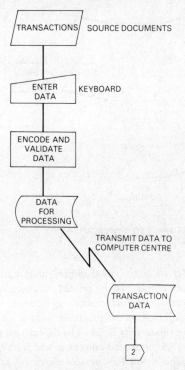

Figure A2 *System flowchart: (a) batch processing – off-line activities – key-to-disc encoding and validation;*

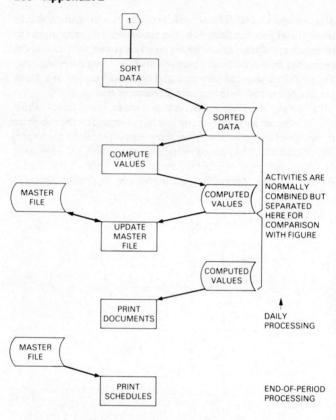

(b) batch processing – processing activities

on the computer monitor (visual display unit) either in text or graphics mode, or output may be printed, in which case either the input/output symbol or report symbol may be used.

If data is transferred to the processor from a file or from the processor to a file this activity is shown by the relevant magnetic tape or disc symbols. All inputs and outputs to and from the processor, represented by the action box, are connected by a horizontal or vertical flowline with arrowheads showing the direction of flow, i.e. in or out of the processor. Each action box should contain a brief 'legend' defining the nature of the activity and each file symbol should be labelled with the name of the file. The nature of the output should also be specified, whether, for instance, it is an error report (i.e. invalid items), audit trail consisting of a list of the transactions posted, a business document such as a payslip, a schedule such as a payroll, or a management report such as a list of items out of stock, or customers whose credit limit is exceeded.

4. Processing activities. As a general guide most systems consist of common types of activity, albeit in different combinations according to specific system features. A standard set of activities particularly appropriate for a batch processing system would consist of:

1. Data recording on source documents or automatic data capture by means of laser scanning of bar codes, factory terminals or auto teller terminals, etc.
2. Data conversion (data preparation) to machine – sensible media, i.e. magnetic tape or disc.
3. Data validation.
4. Sort data to a defined file sequence to facilitate file updating.
5. Compute values.
6. Update files.
7. Print documents.
8. Statistical analysis of data.
9. Print reports.

5. Important principles and concepts in the construction of system flowcharts.

(a) It is important to appreciate that the output from one activity or stage of processing provides the input to the next activity. This is because of the progressive nature in which data is processed from basic facts to final information.

(b) Some flowcharts require several pages and for reasons of continuity an off-page connector symbol is used.

(c) A flowchart must be identifiable and authenticated For this reason it must show clearly the 'name of the system', the 'date' the chart was constructed so that it is possible to assess its status (i.e. whether it is portraying the current system, a future system or an earlier version of the present system), and the 'author' of the chart or system.

(*d*) Some parts of a system are processed daily, weekly, monthly or annually according to circumstances and requirements. A factory payroll system may have daily data capture procedures relating to jobs worked on in the factory with a weekly wages calculation and statistical routine. This may be supported by monthly statistics for management accounting needs The system must also incorporate the annual preparation of certificates of pay, tax deducted and national insurance contributions (P60s).

In some instances the preparation of sales invoices may be

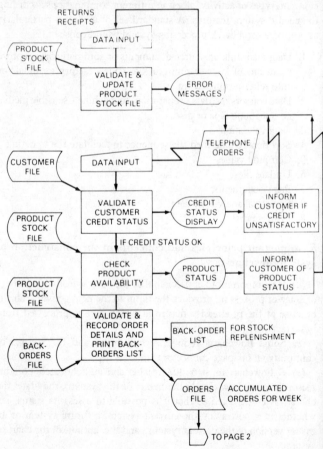

performed daily or weekly according to volume, but statements of account are prepared monthly at the end of the trading period.

In other instances, some parts of a system are performed on-line interactively, as in the instance of inputting sales order details. This is referred to as on-line order entry and is often supported by daily processing of the orders in batch mode. These aspects are illustrated in Fig. A3 which shows a simple flowchart of both on-line and batch processing activities.

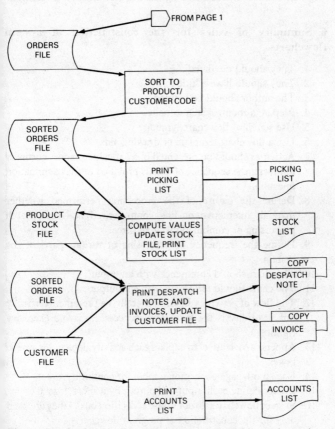

Figure A3 *Combined on-line and batch processing activities: (a) interactive processing; (b) batch processing*

(*e*) Some questions may require a more simplified type of flowchart than those previously discussed, showing the flow of data in the system. In such a case a 'block diagram' may be used – *see* Fig. 13.2 which outlines a payroll system. A block diagram is a low level flowchart for depicting a 'system outline' and includes the system functions, indicating inputs, files used and outputs produced independent of operational details.

(*f*) It is important to appreciate, however, that specific data flow diagrams should be used when a greater degree of detail is required.

6. Summary of rules for the construction of system flowcharts.

1. They should be 'dated'.
2. They should have a 'title'.
3. The author should be 'named'.
4. Prepare a rough sketch initially.
5. Use standard flowchart symbols.
6. Use a flowchart template or drawing aids.
7. Activities should be presented in a logical sequence, normally following the sequence of details provided in the examination question.
8. Define the nature of the processing performed whether manual, interactive on-line computerised activities, batch processing or combinations of all three.
9. Define the frequency of processing of various parts of the system.
10. The chart should commence with an 'input'.
11. The chart should terminate with an 'output'.
12. The flow of activities should generally be presented vertically but flexibility is the keynote of success, i.e. avoid excessive rigidity.
13. Append a 'narrative' to explain each activity depicted in action boxes.
14. Use an off-page connector symbol for continuity.
15. Briefly define each input and output by a short 'legend'.
16. System flowcharts do not utilise a 'decision box' – they are used only for the construction of program flowcharts.
17. Be consistent in the method of chart construction but remember the need for flexibility.

Appendix 3

Case study 1: Wines and spirits wholesaler

1. Question. A wines and spirits wholesaler stocks a range of approximately 400 different lines and delivers by van on regular weekly runs to customers who are mainly off-licences and clubs.

The majority of orders are received by telephone and any one customer may place several orders during the week which must be accumulated and delivered in one consignment. When a customer telephones he expects to be advised of the availability of an item requested and, if not in stock, the alternatives that are available. At present, sales order forms are filled in by the telephone salesmen and sent to the warehouse where they are used for the despatch of the items. Hand-written despatch notes are used as the basis of the invoices which are typed and sent by post sometime later.

Particular problems which arise in the present system are:

(i) Delays and inaccuracies in stock recording mean that a shortage is only discovered when an order is being made up. It is then often too late to discover if a substitute item would be acceptable.

(ii) Occasionally only part of a consignment is delivered because a sales order has been overlooked or not received by Despatch.

(iii) The number of bad debts is rising and the present credit control procedures are inadequate, causing deliveries to be made to bad payers.

(iv) The telephone salesmen at present are only able to act as order takers, whereas the company would like them to play a more active selling and credit control role.

The company is planning to use a microcomputer for its order processing, stock control, sales invoicing and accounting procedures and the configuration envisaged will comprise a processor, disc storage, line printer and several VDUs.

You are required to:

(a) produce a systems flowchart of the new procedures with sufficient narrative to explain each step, taking care to identify

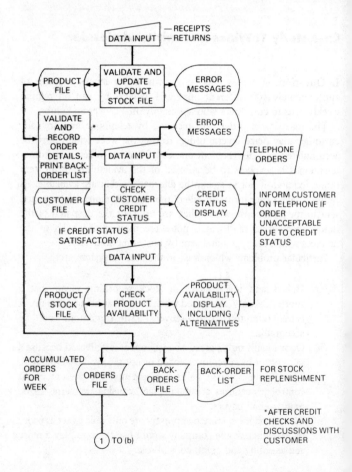

those parts of your system which will be interactive and those that will be run in batch mode;
(b) describe briefly the contents of the main files to be used;
(c) explain briefly how your proposed system will help to overcome the problems experienced with the present method of operation.

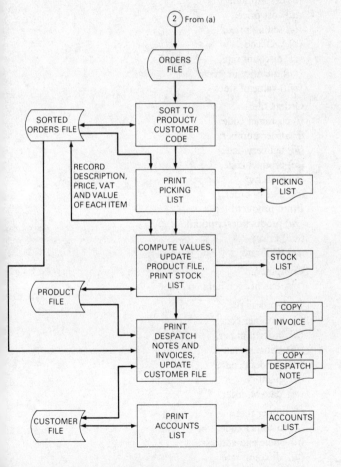

Figure A4 *Systems flowchart, wines and spirits wholesale system: (a) interactive processing; (b) batch processing*

2. Answer.

(a) *Systems flowchart*:

(b) *Contents of main files*:

Product file:

(i) product code;

(ii) description;

(iii) cost price;

(iv) selling price;

(v) VAT code;

(vi) discount rate;

(vii) quantity in stock;

(viii) value of stock.

Orders file:

(i) customer code;

(ii) order number;

(iii) delivery date;

(iv) product code;

(v) quantity;

(vi) date of order;

From product file:

(vii) product description;

(viii) price;

(ix) VAT rate;

Computed:

(x) value of each item on order.

Back-orders file;

(i) customer code;

(ii) order number;

(iii) delivery date;

(iv) product code;

(v) quantity;

(vi) date of order.

Customer file:

(i) customer code;

(ii) name and address;

(iii) discount rate;

(iv) credit limit;

(v) account balance;

(*vi*) account balance age analysis;

(*vii*) area code;

(*viii*) turnover.

(*c*) *Overcoming the problems of the present system.* The analysis which follows is in accordance with the order of details given in the question.

(*i*) *Delays and inaccuracies in stock recording.* Such delays and inaccuracies cause stock shortages which will be eliminated by the VDU operator checking the product file to assess the availability of products in response to customer enquiries on the telephone. If specific items are unavailable or the full order quantity is not in stock then the customer is informed. The VDU operator is then in a position to discuss alternative product lines with the customer while still on the telephone. This means a firm order will still be obtained. If the customer is willing to wait for shortages then these are recorded in a back-order file. A list is also printed for stock replenishment purposes and for controlling order items not yet despatched.

(*ii*) *Part consignments.* Part consignments will be eliminated as sales orders are recorded on the disc orders file immediately they are received from the customer on the telephone. The warehouse despatches orders by means of a picking list produced from the orders file which prevents order details not being received by the warehouse. Previously the sales order forms could go astray. Unfortunately it is difficult to eliminate items being overlooked on the picking list due to human fallibility. This can only be remedied by an independent checker on the despatch deck.

(*iii*) *Bad debts increasing.* Before accepting an order the VDU operator checks the credit status of customers by looking up the accounts on the customer file. The details are displayed on the video screen. By this means the order is rejected immediately and is not recorded on the orders file. The customer is also immediately informed on the telephone that the order cannot be accepted either due to the allowed credit limit being exceeded or payments being overdue.

(*iv*) *Selling and credit control role of salespersons.* The telephone/VDU salespersons will have their responsibilities extended with the new system to include credit control achieved by the routine outlined in (*iii*) above. A more active selling role is accomplished by the routine outlined in (*i*) above.

Case study 2: Car hire company

The following case study is based on a question set by the City and Guilds of London Institute in the 747 paper. The question has been slightly modified.

1. System description. A car hire firm operates a self-drive service from 30 offices throughout the UK, most of them being at airports or main railway stations. Customers may pick up a car at one office and return it to the company at a different office.

At the company's London headquarters is a large computer supporting terminals in each of the offices. Each office terminal consists of a VDU, keyboard and hard-copy printer.

Customers may book cars for hire by telephone, by letter or by calling in person. These booking requests should be addressed at least 3 days in advance to the office where the customer wishes to pick up the car. Since cars may be hired from one office and returned to another, the computer must keep track of the location of each car and what bookings are arranged for it. A minimum of 8 hours is required between bookings for any one car for maintenance. Each car is serviced every 5000 miles, so the computer must keep details of mileages for each car. If an office does not have enough cars at a particular time to cover its bookings then customers are turned away.

You are to design a system to run on this computer configuration to satisfy the following requirements:

(a) *Inputs* (via the keyboard) at each office are:
   (i) *Bookings.* The clerk inputs date and time of collection, date, time and place of returning, size of car required.
   (ii) *Collection.* Hirers pay a deposit on collecting the car. The clerk inputs details of this and confirms to the system that the car is now out on hire.
   (iii) *Return.* Hirers pay the balance of the hire charge on return. The clerk inputs details of this and the car mileage.

(b) *Outputs* required at each office are:
   (i) A twice daily printout showing the bookings so far recorded for that office for the next 72 hours (details of which cars are booked and which cars are due for service).
   (ii) Details of each car can be displayed on the VDU on request

showing current bookings on file, present location, mileage since last service.

(*iii*) Computer-printed confirmation of booking is produced and posted first-class to telephone or postal customers and handed to personal callers.

2. Tasks. The overall requirement of the question is to design a system to satisfy the details provided. A number of tasks are necessary, which are outlined below:

(*a*) As a means of communicating the structure of the proposed system to management, compile a systems flowchart of the system which will be implemented in each of the 30 offices. The interaction of customers, the office and the computer must be clearly shown.

(*b*) Show by means of a block diagram the computer configuration you think would be in use at the London headquarters, indicating how it is connected to each of the 30 offices.

(*c*) Prepare a computer runchart, clearly indicating the input, processing, use of master files, and output at each stage of processing.

(*d*) Define the master files you need to support the system specifying the data elements (fields), data type and the size of each element of data.

3. Solution.

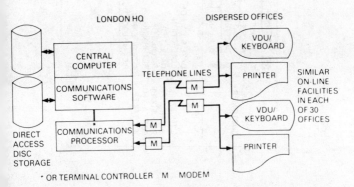

(*a*)

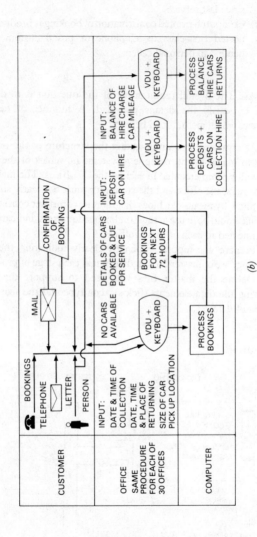

(b)

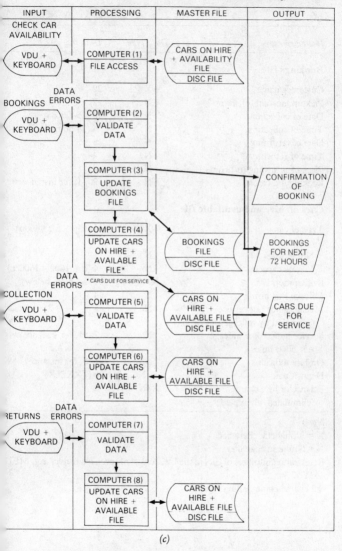

INPUT	PROCESSING	MASTER FILE	OUTPUT

CHECK CAR AVAILABILITY
VDU + KEYBOARD ↔ COMPUTER (1) FILE ACCESS ↔ CARS ON HIRE + AVAILABILITY FILE DISC FILE

BOOKINGS DATA ERRORS
VDU + KEYBOARD ↔ COMPUTER (2) VALIDATE DATA

COMPUTER (3) UPDATE BOOKINGS FILE → CONFIRMATION OF BOOKING

COMPUTER (4) UPDATE CARS ON HIRE + AVAILABLE FILE* ↔ BOOKINGS FILE DISC FILE → BOOKINGS FOR NEXT 72 HOURS
*CARS DUE FOR SERVICE

COLLECTION DATA ERRORS
VDU + KEYBOARD ↔ COMPUTER (5) VALIDATE DATA ↔ CARS ON HIRE + AVAILABLE FILE DISC FILE → CARS DUE FOR SERVICE

COMPUTER (6) UPDATE CARS ON HIRE + AVAILABLE FILE ↔ CARS ON HIRE + AVAILABLE FILE DISC FILE

RETURNS DATA ERRORS
VDU + KEYBOARD ↔ COMPUTER (7) VALIDATE DATA

COMPUTER (8) UPDATE CARS ON HIRE + AVAILABLE FILE ↔ CARS ON HIRE + AVAILABLE FILE DISC FILE

(c)

Figure A5 *Case study solution: (a) block diagram of computer configuration; (b) system flowchart; (c) computer runchart; (d) content and structure of master files*

(d)

Data element	Data type	Data size
Bookings file		
Customer name	X	20
Pick up location (office no.)	N	2
Date of collection	N	8 (25/06/85)
Time of collection	N	4 (24 hour clock)
Date of returning	N	8
Time of returning	N	4
Place of returning (office no.)	N	2
Booking indicator	N	2 (–1, for instance)★
Cars on hire and available file		
Type of car	X	1 (e.g. S for saloon)
Size of car:		
No. of seats	N	1
Engine capacity	N	4 (e.g. 1600 = 1600cc)
Registration No.	X/N	7 (*see* Note below)
Mileage this hiring	N	4
Mileage since last service (increased by mileage this hiring)	N	4
Service indicator if mileage = > 5000 miles	N	2 (+1, for instance)★
On hire indicator	N	1 (0, for instance)
Deposit paid	X/N	6 (£XX.XX)
Balance of hire charge (eliminated when paid)	X/N	6

Notes

X = Alphabetic character

N = Numeric character

Registration numbers of cars in the UK consist of seven characters, e.g. MFD 443Y.

★2 characters including sign

Index

M&E Handbooks

Law

Business and Management

Advanced Economics/G L Thirkettle
Advertising/F Jefkins
Applied Economics/E Seddon, J D S Appleton
Basic Economics/G L Thirkettle
Business Administration/L Hall
Business and Financial Management/B K R Watts
Business Organisation/R R Pitfield
Business Mathematics/L W T Stafford
Business Systems/R G Anderson
Business Typewriting/S F Parks
Computer Science/J K Atkin
Data Processing Vol 1: Principles and Practice/R G Anderson
Data Processing Vol 2: Information Systems and Technology/R G Anderson
Economics for 'O' Level/L B Curzon
Elements of Commerce/C O'Connor
Human Resources Management/H T Graham
Industrial Administration/J C Denyer, J Batty
International Marketing/L S Walsh
Management, Planning and Control/R G Anderson
Management – Theory and Principles/T Proctor
Managerial Economics/J R Davies, S Hughes
Marketing/G B Giles
Marketing Overseas/A West
Marketing Research/T Proctor, M A Stone
Microcomputing/R G Anderson
Modern Commercial Knowledge/L W T Stafford
Modern Marketing/F Jefkins
Office Administration/J C Denyer, A L Mugridge
Operational Research/W M Harper, H C Lim
Organisation and Methods/R G Anderson
Production Management/H A Harding
Public Administration/M Barber, R Stacey
Public Relations/F Jefkins
Purchasing/C K Lysons
Sales and Sales Management/P Allen
Statistics/W M Harper
Stores Management/R J Carter

Accounting and Finance

Auditing/L R Howard
Basic Accounting/J O Magee
Basic Book-keeping/J O Magee
Capital Gains Tax/V Di Palma
Company Accounts/J O Magee
Company Secretarial Practice/L Hall, G M Thom
Cost and Management Accounting – Vols 1 & 2/W M Harper
Elements of Banking/D P Whiting
Elements of Finance for Managers/B K R Watts
Elements of Insurance/D S Hansell
Finance of Foreign Trade/D P Whiting
Investment: A Practical Approach/D Kerridge
Practice of Banking/E P Doyle, J E Kelly
Principles of Accounts/E F Castle, N P Owens
Taxation/H Toch

Humanities and Science

Biology Advanced Level/P T Marshall
British Government and Politics/F Randall
Chemistry for 'O' Level/G Usher
Economic Geography/H Robinson
European History 1789–1914/C A Leeds
Geology/A W R Potter, H Robinson
Introduction to Ecology/J C Emberlin
Land Surveying/R J P Wilson
Modern Economic History/E Seddon
Political Studies/C A Leeds
Sociology 'O' Level/F Randall
Twentieth Century History 1900–45/C A Leeds
World History: 1900 to the Present Day/C A Leeds